Praise for Between Now and When

"A mind-expanding, well-written narrative that intrigues on both a story level and a metaphysical one. Read this book. Have your mind blown. Understand the universe."

—Marc Darrow, author of *Shrinking the Truth*

"Through his own personal magical mystery tour, Dr. House opens the doors to the hidden realities that shape our familiar world. An honest, unflinching account of one man's extraordinary spiritual journey."

—Henry Jacoby, PhD, Department of Philosophy and Religious Studies, East Carolina University

BETWEEN
NOW AND
WHEN

BETWEEN
NOW AND
WHEN

How My Death
Made My Life Worth Living

A TRUE STORY

RICHARD HOUSE, MD

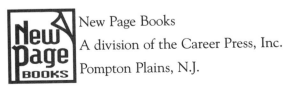

New Page Books
A division of the Career Press, Inc.
Pompton Plains, N.J.

BETWEEN NOW AND WHEN
EDITED AND TYPESET BY KARA KUMPEL
Cover design by Howard Grossman/12E Design
Printed in the U.S.A.

To order this title, please call toll-free 1-800-CAREER-1 (NJ and
Canada: 201-848-0310) to order using VISA or MasterCard, or for further information on books from Career Press.

The Career Press, Inc.
220 West Parkway, Unit 12
Pompton Plains, NJ 07444
www.careerpress.com
www.newpagebooks.com

Library of Congress Cataloging-in-Publication Data
CIP Data Available Upon Request.

This book is dedicated to the mysterious young man who touched my elbow in Victoria Gardens, Calcutta, and to Meher Baba, who made him do it.

Befitting a fortunate slave,
Follow every command of the master
Without regard to why or what.

About what you hear from the master,
Never say it is wrong, because my dear,
The fault lies in your own incapacity to understand him.

Having been released from ignorance,
I am slave of the master whose every action
Is for the greatest benefit of all concerned.
—Hafiz

Acknowledgments

Putting a worthy story into readable form is no small task. It takes a cadre of dedicated people to finish what a pencil and a few legal pads started a few years back.

This read owes its birth to Teresa Poole, PhD, who not only typed the manuscript, but also offered valuable editorial comments along the way. Thank you.

Mike Sirota, editor-at-large, a wonderful guy, deserve a golden nod. He convinced me to finally get a computer and smart phone. Somewhere along the line, he became a good friend as he whipped this work into shape. Thanks, Mike.

It was Eric Evans, my tech guy, who launched me into cyberspace and made all this possible. I appreciate it, Eric. Also on my thank-you list is Kathie Colburn, who after first reading this work was moved to tears.

And, of course, New Page Books/Career Press provided the wherewithal and expertise to send this story out to the world. Special thanks to editors Kirsten Dalley and Kara Kumpel, who did a wonderful job marshalling this book into print. The entire crew at New Page were a delight to work with. Thanks, all.

Contents

Introduction

Mostly, life on Earth is a pretty consistent slog of daily concerns mixed with occasional sparks of the divine. We live for those extraordinary moments when all is well, when God is in His heaven and we are filled with peace.

But it is true that many of us suffer enormously, our circumstances beyond control and painful to experience, the sparks of the divine infrequent or missing altogether. Is the colossal game of God and man rational or even reasonable? This question is one that each of us must answer in our own way—moreover, it requires help from beyond.

The following story relates my own quest for answers that led me on a journey that was both an inner one and one that had me traipsing around the world: Hawaii, Fiji, Australia, India, London, and, eventually, New York. The springboard for my quest was a near-death experience that came after a long partnership with Jack Daniels. I found myself in the emergency room of my own hospital, the doctor now a dying patient. I was 33 years old at the time, and it did not entirely surprise me to be on death's doorstep. Something, a Mystical Voice, had spoken to me as a teenager and said that I would indeed die at that age.

Clearly, there is more to the story than an early death would afford—and there is much more to it than a search for serenity in 12-step recovery.

Good Lord! I was taken by the hand on a magical journey that led me on forays into beautiful dimensions that I didn't dream could exist. Also, it came to my attention that my quest had purpose in mind: the mysteries unveiled came with obligations attached. Moreover, along the way I stumbled upon the hidden mechanisms of earthly life—*metaphysics*, as it were, that organize human and cosmic energies. I discovered that the Earth itself has energy centers much like we do, with channels of energetic flow that make up a planetary grid.

So, this is a story of transcendence—yes, and discovery as well. Perhaps I should say that the real fuel for my quest, my journey, was Love—the human sort that so enlivens life on Earth, as well as the divine love that underwrites all human experience. Love is what unlocks the clanging doors of personal limitation and allows entry into the boundless dimensions that are described in the pages that follow.

I hope that you find something in this story that unlocks your personal doors, something far more precious than serenity: radiant love that erases worry and suffering, that can even lead you to the wondrous land that I discovered, the one that exists right here, right now.

Chapter One
Cloistered in Paradise

Meditation is the action of silence.
—Jiddu Krishnamurti

"Ca-Ca Street? Do I really want to live on Ca-Ca Street?" I ask this question of a bantam rooster who is eyeing me first with one eye and then the other. He obviously lives somewhere close by and seems unoffended by the street name as he goes pecking about.

The clapboard duplex across the street is the only rental available in the town of Kapaa, Kauai, Hawaii, where, with some effort, destiny has plopped me down. Still, I'm hesitant. After trashing a perfectly good life as a doctor and family man, I expected more from the universe than this humble dwelling promises.

The door to unit B is open and I can see the middle-aged *haole* landlord inside. He's up on a ladder fiddling with a light fixture and hasn't noticed me yet. We *haoles* are white folks, often from California, who are trying to make a go of it in Hawaii. *Haole* is a pejorative term of sorts that denotes our position as second-class citizens—a novel experience for most of us—and we never outgrow the label.

"Aloha," I say, with some enthusiasm.

"Hi," he responds, whereupon I resolve not to use this greeting unless it comes at me first. "Interested?" he asks, as I look around—no furniture, linoleum floor, stained kitchen sink, and a small bedroom with an overhead fan. I decide not to brave a look into the bathroom.

"Yes," I reply, and nod as he names the monthly rent. *Yes, I'll take the sonofabitch, even if it's on Ca-Ca Street.*

He turns to me and points to the stove. "It'll take a week or so to get a working stove installed," he said, handing me his business card. "Why don't you call me then if you still want it?" As I turned and walked away, the rooster crowed three times. *Gotta be a sign*, I think. Of what, I can't imagine.

What I do know is that at age 35 I've escaped the prophecy I'd been given of death at 33 and am healthier than I have any right to be. It's more than a second chance at life, the gift sometimes given to fools or drunks. Much more. The Presence that seems to be orchestrating my journey, this *Mystical Voice*, appears to have more in mind than redemptive work. The magical experiences that have brought me to this island paradise are so enlivening that I really don't care much about the things that used to drive my behavior, such as money, prestige, success, or even the friends and family I've left behind—my daughter, Megan, the only exception. Thank God she's only 2 and doesn't yet experience the anguish of separation that I do.

❧

The next day I leave my expensive motel room and begin walking to the Kountry Kitchen, an unlikely diner catering to *haoles*. The plumeria trees are in full bloom with the lilting fragrance of frangipani competing with whiffs of dog shit as I pass the backyards of *locals*, the people of Hawaii who are not *haoles*. Over coffee, I again scan the island paper for rentals and find one new listing, a condo at Pono Kai, a hundred dollars more per month, *but it's right on the beach.* I pick up the pay phone and call the agent. "I'll take it, sight unseen."

Pona Kai, I discover, is a new resort set on a sheltered cove near Kapaa. The condo still has the smell of new carpet and new rattan furniture. The small ground-level patio fronts a grassy area where I stand looking at the beach that is perhaps 50 yards away. There are long-needle Japanese pines that partially obscure the view of tourists playing in the gentle surf. The brilliant blue sea is calm this day, a gentle breeze bringing sounds of laughter my way. I love it. Thanks, Voice, whoever the hell you are.

I reenter the one-bedroom condo through the sliding screen door and sit at the kitchen table with the sound of the breaking waves still quite audible. I watch as people wander about, some going down to the beach and others walking along the asphalt path that parallels the row of Japanese pines going right to left along the sandy shore. I can hardly believe my good fortune. It is January 4, 1981, and I happily sign a six-month lease. I have found a home in paradise.

I put the intrusive TV in a closet but arrange to have a phone installed the next day. Some intrusion is going to be necessary. I then place a straight-backed chair near the sliding glass door just behind the drawn curtains to the left, and sit. The first meditation is so deep and blissful that, after 20 minutes, I feel absorbed into the very fabric of Kauai, the magical essence of the place now a part of my being—such beauty, such peace. It is the sound of the myna birds outside that pulls me back to the lesser reality of day-to-day life.

I stand up and clap my hands three times, announcing to my unseen captain, the being who has been orchestrating my life, *I'm here. I'm here. Let's get on with it.*

The next day, I pick up the newly installed phone and call the island hospital for an appointment with the administrator, Mr. Connor. He will be happy to see me today, so I put on a pair of khakis and a white shirt and pull on my cowboy boots—for the last time, I hope. I ride the 10 miles in a taxi with Duke Ellington playing. The local driver's only comment: "Love big band." I certainly believe him and hope that my Harley will arrive soon.

Mr. Connor listens to my ideas for starting a rehab clinic on Kauai, where there currently is none. I lay out the scheme for him: a 20-bed facility tied in with 12-step recovery, with me as medical director. He nods attentively and asks appropriate questions. "I'll present this idea to the board and get back to you," he says, as he rises to shake my hand. His expression is so unrevealing that I really can't tell what he thinks of the prospects, but at least the idea is on the table.

Kelly, my AA friend from Sierra Madre, is arriving the next day, so while I'm in town I rent a car.

Kelly, tall, attractive, and quite thin, has her camera with her; she's a professional photographer, among other things. I'm delighted to see her, and her visit gives us a good excuse to play tourist and do some sightseeing. We travel the island from Waimea Beach to the west, Poipou to the south, then Hanalei to the north beyond Princeville. It is here that we stop for a meal at the Tiki Bar and listen to a Hawaiian band yodeling while we are enjoying mahi mahi fresh from the sea. Farther north we find the Tokay trail head and a small general store where a resident *haole* couple regales us with stories of hikers who start up, but never return.

"They's still out there somewhere, wandering around naked and living off the land," the fellow says. Kelly looks at me with eyebrows raised as she snaps a few pictures. The feel of the place is just spooky enough to make the story believable. There is a dense mist in the air that seems to enter our bones and dampen our previously upbeat spirits.

Driving south, we both laugh at the dark feeling that has now passed, the sunshine brightening our mood as we arrive at Kapaa and splash around in the turbulent surf. The week passes with a suddenness that reminds me that all good things do so, and that I'm not here to be a lay-on-the-beach tourist. Time to get on with the program.

Kelly having returned to the mainland, I get serious about my true work: reengaging with spirit through meditation. I sit behind the drawn curtain and let my mind float like a bobbing beach ball on the surface of the sea. This becomes my main activity for the next six months in spite of the alluring beauty on the other side of the closed curtains. It is only later that I understand why Spirit directed me to this spot. At the time, I had no understanding of the infrastructure of the creation—a.k.a the universe; the whole ball of wax—metaphysics, as it were. There are, it turns out, three general types of energy manifest in it: causal, subtle, and visible (gross).

The highest, most powerful energy is *causal*, or mental, deriving from the mental dimension that is actually a world in itself, the seat of the archangels. The dream of Isa, the Divine Mother, filters down through this world and acquires form via causal vectors called Universal Sanskaras. Sanskaras, if I may borrow from the Hinduism Dictionary, are the imprints left on the subconscious mind by experience in this or previous lives, which then color all of life, one's nature, responses, states of mind, and so on. These sans-karas are directive and descend to the next level of manifestation, the *subtle* world of energy, also a dimensional world ruled by the host of angels. The directive, causal sanskaras are energized while passing through the various levels of the subtle world to become subtle sanskaras, which then acquire various gradations of density to order all that occurs in the *visible* creation. The gross world is made up of dense energy based on *gross sanskaras*, the actual blue-prints that order all earthly events.

Most people are only conscious of the visible, gross world. There does come a time when every soul, including you, dear reader, through dint of effort or the grace of God, or both, begins to di-rectly experience the higher dimensions. This is the beginning of the true spiritual journey or quest that eventually brings the soul to God's doorstep, the threshold of union.

Did I understand any of this at the time? No. I had no idea at all. I was, however, beginning to experience the subtle world, my magical, beautiful land where there are no worries and no fear. This was incentive enough to get me to push away ordinary pur-suits (and the TV) in favor of sitting in a straight-backed chair behind a curtain in paradise.

I would also learn that the subtle world of such beauty and power is more accessible on islands and also specific locations scat-tered around the world. Other favorable geographic spots for ac-cessing higher consciousness are mountaintops or deep canyons where the hubbub of the gross world is faint. Much like a board game, aspirants are often moved by Spirit from one spot to another to allow for expansion of consciousness; this is called the spiritual path, the quest, a journey inspired from within when the conscious mind is sufficiently prepared—and quieted to allow Spirit to lead.

I begin each day well before dawn with a quick shower and cup of tea. To follow, a brisk walk along the asphalt path that extends the length of the resort and thence into the residential neighborhoods.

In the predawn darkness, the sea remains a vast black expanse that marks Earthly time with the sound of breaking waves—music to my ears. In the neighborhoods to the left of Pono Kai are the humble houses of the locals, whose dogs note my passing with half-hearted barks. To the right of the resort flows an inland river that begins its journey in the distant mountains, joining the sea just beyond the footbridge that spans it near Pono Kai. I often stop on the bridge as dawn brings color to the sea and sky and watch the commercial fishermen ready their boats, mostly handmade, for the day's work far from land. Their guttural shouts as they call to one another, mostly in mock exasperation at the clumsiness of their crews, liven up the misty beginning of my day which, thereafter, will be silent and still.

Each day I sit in meditation, waiting. For what, I don't actually know, but each meditation brings something novel to my damp-ened mind. Bursts of color and light sometimes come forth behind my closed eyes, but mostly it is *nothing* that I experience, a nothing that is somehow alive and expectant and never dull. After 20 min-utes or longer, I pull out and attend to daily tasks, perhaps walking to the Big Save to buy groceries or making necessary phone calls to the mainland where my old life still has persistent, long-distance demands.

All through the day and night I return to the chair for sessions, as many as 10 or 12 in 24 hours, each meditation a connection to *something* that is prying me open like a blade inserted into an oys-ter shell where perhaps a pearl may be hidden. And thus a routine is struck, a daily mixture of the usual and mystical that finds me isolated and sequestered for the most part, stepping into the outside world when necessary. I don't read or listen to music—no TV, no movies, no distractions of any sort.

My Harley, I discover, has been lost in transit when its destina-tion was switched from Maui to Kauai, so I am on foot until further

notice—not a bad thing at all, I discover. All goes slower and qui-
eter, and it is good.

One morning I am up at 2 a.m., the night sky filled with starry
pinpoints, clusters of diamonds that have entranced mankind since
the beginning of time. I am standing on my porch in between sessions when I hear distant caravan bells tinkling far out to sea. How
can this be? I can almost see the beasts of burden and their jolting
wagons as they slowly traverse the night sky in an impossible tableau. I shake my head as the tinkling bells gradually fade, the caravan gone on to other starlit venues. Such things may not easily submit to logical thought, but the experience is a real one nonetheless.

The second such thing occurs a few nights later. This time the
starry sky is filled with the sound of a chorus singing. The complex
music of Mozart comes drifting to me as I stand spellbound, my
bare feet on the cool sand of the beach. The singing is so perfectly
intoned that it cannot be of human origin, even as my human ears
record it. Angels? I had heard it said that Mozart turned his cupped
ear to the heavens to find his inspiration, hearing the celestial
sounds of angelic music that he endeavored to bring to earth for us
all to experience. I *believe* it as I listen to the night sky on the island
of Kauai, a gift of Spirit that I will always cherish.

A few mornings later, I awaken on the couch to the light of day,
an unusual departure from the daily routine of arising before dawn.
Even more disturbing is the mood that greets me—a depressive
feeling of hopelessness that I'd never experienced before. I sit bolt
upright as my heart first races in panic and then slows to a fearful
slog. Not just a mood, this gloom has substance and definition, as
if I have entered a horrific land of despair and death from which
there is no escape. Moments pass before I can muster the courage
to throw off the tendrils of fear that have glued me to the couch.

One step at a time, I walk outside to the porch and am shocked to see huge land crabs with bleached legs and mottled pink bodies, all with their tentacled eyes fixed on me, many of them out on the grass in hellish clusters, all of them sentient creatures who have come forward to view this intruder who perhaps doesn't belong on their turf.

The automatic sprinklers come on, as they do each morning, and the spidery things scuttle off, leaving me standing there, gaze fixed on the familiar scene of tall pine trees, the beach, and the ocean that extends out to the curved horizon, no clouds in the sky. What keeps me rooted to the spot is the growing awareness that the beauty before me is fake, a visual illusion, a perception that has no objective existence, a postcard view in flat 2-D that hovers before my eyes without entering my soul. This scene of paradise is empty; it is a paradise lost, an illusion shattered.

The dark, depressive state is the first that I have ever experienced. What have I done to incur it? Nothing. It just came: unannounced, unsolicited—and unwanted. I hate it. A hot shower doesn't help. Where has all the music gone?

I sit in the chair but can't connect in any meaningful way and, after a few such sessions, I gather my resolve and walk to the Big Save for a rare lunch at the cafeteria there: white rice with a fried egg and thin beef patty on top, with liberal squirts of soy sauce and hot chili sesame oil. This dish, called egg-on by the locals, is cheap and surprisingly tasty. Not so this day. My taste buds are as dead as the rest of me. As I scan my fellow diners, mostly locals, I blink away tears that flow of their own volition, prompting my abrupt exit. I walk back home, where I am fearful that land crabs might greet me—might even eat me. The air is laced with glutinous webs of fear that I brush aside as I walk the familiar path back to the condo. Thank God, no land crabs.

A day passes, then another, just as vile as the last. On the third morning I leap off the couch, my spirits revived and soaring like graceful seabirds in flight. I feel light as a feather, renewed and fresh, the memory of the last few days fading into the nightmarish past. *No more will I visit that awful place*, I think. Instead I will live in bliss and grace forevermore.

I spend the next wonderful day alternately sitting in the chair and walking on the beach, the bright sun clearing the cobwebs that had clouded my mind. I celebrate by walking to Kapaa to stand in line with Japanese women at the fish market. After the doors open, we each in turn examine the slices of ahi, yellowtail tuna, for cut and price, each transaction accompanied by gestures and comments from the fishmonger. The day's catch soon gone, the doors close once again. That evening, I pan-fry the ahi in garlic butter, a special treat to celebrate euphoric release from despair. But it is not to last.

Two days later I again awake in the clutches of gray gloom and hopelessness, all merriment gone. This second episode makes it quite clear that the bipolar swings are independent of any direct causation—that it is somehow connected to my spiritual quest, my meditative practice, and as such must be borne. It is, nonetheless, suffering of the highest order, an unexpected reversal of the magic that has brought me to this point—it is hell after heaven, misery after surrendering my life to the call of Spirit.

The rollercoaster ride goes on for days and days, the mountain-top experience of euphoria devolving to the depressive depths of mental anguish. I start writing notes to myself when feeling bright and cheerful—*Buck-up my friend, it will pass*—and leaving the notes within clutching distance of the couch where I sleep.

All attempts at control of this process eventually fail. Nothing that I do is of any help when I am in the pit of scummy despair. One such night, I decide to give up the fight. I hurry out of the condo at midnight and run along the path to the left, eventually reaching the dissolute neighborhood where barking dogs hold sway.

A soaking rain pouring down, I stop. I stop and raise my face to the heavens and yell, "Okay! I can take it, give me more!" I sink to my knees, tears and the rain forming pools of glistening water around me.

That was the end of it, my friend. No more swings—the ride was over. My surrender was the key, the process itself a surgical excision of volatility of mood; the result, unshakeable emotional stability from that day to the present.

And there was more, a lot more, but before getting into it, the question arises, how did I get to this island paradise? How did it all begin? It began with prison, a metaphorical jail perhaps, but the bars of steel seemed quite real—and, in fact, they were...

Chapter Two

Here on Earth

Something began me
And it had no beginning
Something will end me
And it has no end
—Carl Sandburg

October, 1973

Where am I? The rough wool blanket, a shade of dingy gray, serves to remind me that Parker Center, the Los Angeles city jail, does not provide amenities of note, and that I am lying on a cot in the on-call room of the jail dispensary. *Oh God,* I think as I struggle awake. The booking area and dispensary are next to the heavy metal door that serves as an entrance to purgatory, if not hell itself. Cops and perps are admitted with a buzz and click, voices loudly raised in perp complaint or perhaps the celebratory cop cheer of a good night's work—sometimes both. It is a never-ending parade of the city's finest and the city's worst, a sensory blast from humanity that calls me back to Earth from wherever it is that I go when asleep.

The second question, *Who am I?* brings a few moments of confusion as my mind sorts out the flood of thoughts that vie for immediate attention. The twilight of sudden awakening delivers me into the world of clanging doors and yelling cops against my will. But, I now know what to call myself: *Dr. Dick*, a collection of experiences, abilities, and good deeds done that have brought me the job of moonlighting jail physician. I had been far away in some dreamland where there was gentle life and easy time, where there was no insistence on duty or painful thinking of this and that.

"Doc," I hear for the second time, the first such call being entwined with that recently abandoned dream. "Come on, we got one." It is Mike yelling through the door, the paunchy, middle-aged nurse in white scrubs who runs the dispensary just as the guards run the prison floors above, with absolute, unquestioned authority. "Doc!" a third time.

The *Who am I?* needs a little more time to settle in before I am ready for my shoes to hit the floor. Oh, yes, I sleep with my shoes on during these awful shifts in the dead of night; white shoes, the sort required at the county hospital where I will soon report for a day shift as well. I put my white-clad feet on the floor and sit up.

"Okay, Mike!" I yell. There is a polished metal mirror in the call room that entices me to flip on the light switch. A blast of fluorescent blue light illuminates my sleep-tossed hair and sagging handlebar mustache. The wax has melted a bit, but a few twists has me looking like a riverboat gambler once again, slicked-back hair and all.

Who am I? indeed.

❧

The first time I remember struggling awake on Earth was at about 7 years of age. Mother called me Richard then. Looking back at it now, there was only the barest inkling of the unusual nature of my life to follow. True, I did have visions of *things* that had nothing to do with the Earth or normalcy, but my 7-year-old self had no way of knowing that such things were rare or weird. A lingering memory of that time comes flooding in as I stand looking at myself in the jail mirror. *I remember the smell of diesel fuel carried on wisps of dense fog as I find myself trudging along with Father between long rows of orange trees hung with fruit imperiled by frost. The smudge pots, taller than I, puff out black smoke that, combined with the cloying fragrance of orange blossom, creates a complex symphony of emotion that plunges deep into my young soul.* I remember this scene with such clarity that it seems like just yesterday. Even now the smell of diesel fuel takes me back to that distant day. I must be smelling the exhaust of the paddy wagon idling outside the jail, waiting to disgorge its nightly catch of lost souls.

Dad, a well-meaning guy, was not exactly my buddy while growing up, more a father, as it were. He was an accomplished dentist who took over his own father's dental practice, located in a renovated horse barn on Floral Avenue in Whittier, California. I remember the red barn with mysterious dental innards and the two tall deodar cedars that Granddad planted next to it on his first day of work. It was under one of the tall deodar cedars that one day I discovered a new answer to the *Who am I?* question that so bothered me even as a 7-year-old kid. One hot summer afternoon I am standing outside of the house on Floral Avenue with fragrant tangerine blossoms filling the still air with magical scent. What happens then is a surprising and sudden awareness, a bolt from a different dimension that suffuses me with awareness of purest identity: *I am.* As I stand rooted to the ground breathing in and then out, in and then out, *I am* is the full blast of self-knowing that pushes aside *7-year-old boy*, that pushes aside *Richard*, and stands all alone, a forever thing of perfection: *me*. I have no word for this thing of perfection that is me. My lips struggle to form my new name, my true identity. What comes forth is *Ichen*. That is the Self of me.

This knowing comes with the exquisite flavor and scent of existence itself, vaguely of lemon and mint with an undertone of rancid oil and noxious sulfur, a complex smell that is *real*. This experience is me, Ichen (Ick'n), on Earth as a boy—Richard, perhaps, but better tongued as Ichen, which I then call myself from that day to the next, and to the next as well.

Mother bends down to peer at me. "*Ichen?*"

A nod from me as I boyishly demur in the face of raised eyebrows above her thick glasses, which magnify her disapproval of my sudden departure from good sense.

"Yes, Ichen." My brave retort sends plumes of blue light and bliss out to the universe, ever expanding, even as I take in her stern countenance, which broadcasts her unwillingness to brook such foolishness, especially in her eldest son. Mom—Ruth Adele Smith, as she was known before marriage—is a no-nonsense gal who is far smarter than most. Our battle of wills is soon decided in her favor as she stands before me, hands on hips, her mind cranking away, her head turning side to side.

I revert to Richard, or Dick if you prefer. Ichen, this mysterious essence, has to be tucked away in the deepest depths of my mental catacombs where I can still feel my Self as pure untrammeled existence. I am nonetheless Richard House, born on the 21st day of December, the winter solstice, in the year of our Lord, 1945.

The net result for my 7-year-old self was that I experienced dual identification as a boy, with dark brown hair, brown eyes, large front teeth, and notable ears, wearing stiff blue jeans with reinforced knees, a striped T-shirt, and a smile—even as I experienced my Self as *Ichen*, the ancient, all-inclusive ocean of existence that I would later have reason to call God Almighty.

❧

My current circumstances don't reflect God's presence at all. Usually the jail dispensary smells of rubbing alcohol and floor polish, but as I respond to Mike's entreaties, I smell cheap red wine exhaled on the breath of the current detainee strapped to the exam table. *Hmm, I know this man: Ernesto.* He has once again run afoul of the laws that govern this fair city. His booking charge, I note, is 647-F, drunk in a public place, unable to care for self or property.

"What is it, Mike?" I ask. Mike is standing at the partially opened door leading out to the hallway and briefly turns his attention to me.

"He says his belly hurts, poor thing."

"He said that last time," I reply, knowing full well that it doesn't matter. Mike returns to his conversation with the cop outside in the noisy hallway without responding to my clever assessment of the situation. I am awake now at 4 a.m.

"Does it hurt here, Ernesto?" I ask in gringo Spanish.

"*Sí.*"

"How about here?"

"*Sí.*"

"And here?"

"*Sí, me duele,*" he says with a grimace. My job is to make certain that he is not suffering from a true malady that would call for hospitalization instead of a few hours in the drunk tank.

"Okay, Mike, give him an ASA and book him," I say. Mike nods in assent, having diagnosed Ernesto's true condition from afar.

No, this isn't Ernesto's first appearance at Parker Center. In fact, many of our nightly clientele are regular members of the "revolving door," the name an earnest reporter gave to the city's policy of jailing our skid row friends and then turning them loose at 5 a.m. after a square, their only reliable meal of the day. Back again they come, Ernesto and his friends, a nightly routine of fortified red wine and jailhouse blues.

As I sit on a metal stool watching Ernesto snore, his jailer not yet arrived, I see the dusky color of his lips and wonder how his internal organs can abide the low oxygen content of his port-wine blood. Maybe he's 50, maybe 40...who knows? Least of all him.

My shift doesn't end until 8 a.m. but Mike usually lets me go early—as long as I complete my rounds doling out meds to misdemeanor and felony detainees, each group of miscreants contained on its own floor above. This is the most onerous part of duty, the thick metal doors along the way buzzing and clicking me into a suburb of hell. "Doc," I hear in dissipated synchrony. "Doc, gimme a 3," or "Doc, I got shakes." *So do I*, I think.

The metal bars enclose dormitory-style rooms with bunks and commodes, inmates snaking up to the bars in front in a sick-call conga line—a noisy one. It wasn't these criminals that I worried about, but rather those that remained horizontal in their bunks and didn't make the most of this medical opportunity. Fortunately, the jailers usually had some idea about their charges, but occasionally I would have to enter the gates of perdition and look for signs of life among the left-behind on bunks.

The smell. A cross of rancid and rank with the carrier fragrance of Pine-Sol. Once I'm inside the cage itself, the door clanks shut behind me, and the fluorescent lights cannot illuminate the darkness I encounter. Dank and scary, these forays into hell enter my dreams with some regularity—dark dreams that spread themselves out over several years afterward.

This was my world for 12 nighttime hours every fourth night for three years. I can't say that I loved it, but the relief of being able to leave it at shift's end, this earthly prison of mine, was exquisite each and every time. I wish that I could have escaped from the more formidable emotional prison as easily, the one with bars of fear and worry.

After changing into my street clothes, white shoes notwithstanding, I head for the County Hospital and a quick shower.

Catherine, my wife, and I actually lived at the hospital in married staff quarters a few hurried steps from the action. She didn't like it. I couldn't blame her for such a sensible reaction to our circumstances, but I loved the bloody work that took me away from her. Judged by my own lights, I was a great intern, a fact later proved by the certificate of excellence that I was awarded at the end of that hellish year. I was a good husband, too, but there was no proof of that, with increasing evidence to the contrary. Oh yes, I did drink a lot, but the real problem was that Catherine had an *artistic temperament* that didn't mesh well with the blood-and-guts life that I presented her. That morning, when I walked into our small apartment on the fifth floor of the intern's residence, she was already gone, probably stuck in freeway traffic on her way to work at Cal-Arts.

I picture her driving and singing show tunes from *The Fantasticks*, her favorite show ever since playing a starring role in it while we were at Butler together during our romantic period: *Soon it's going to rain I can feel it, soon it's going to rain, I can tell...*

I shake off these musical memories and sprint to work in bloody hell where I belong.

I met Catherine at the freshman mixer at Butler University in the magical year of 1963. The Beatles were providing the soundtrack for JFK's Camelot, a mixed metaphor if ever there was one. It was an exciting time as the '60s abrogated American culture in favor of the *Magical Mystery Tour* that took us down paths of discovery filled with the hallucinogenic promise of free love and leftist revolt. I loved it, and I also loved Catherine at first sight. She was tall and lithe with a ballerina's long neck, her brown hair drawn into a tight bun. She glanced and pranced and captivated my heart with consummate ease. It took no effort, whatsoever. She hailed from Erie, Pennsylvania, and chose Butler as one of two universities that offered a master's degree in dance, the idea being that one day she might teach, the stage careers of dancers being notably short and rarely sweet.

I was hopelessly and foolishly in love, the sort of love that has to be tragic at some point, a notion that I probably sensed even then. The heart, as we all know, has an agenda quite separate from logic, or in my case, good sense. A dancer? I should have found another pre-dent (yes, pre-dent) student to idolize and love. That would have been proper, logical, and probably boring, too. It is this rapturous abandonment to *emotion* that gives me the first sense of not being in control of my life in ways that really matter. I am stuck with it and very happy to tolerate whatever negative consequences might follow. I am young, smart, from a good family, and above all, *earnest.* I can manage whatever cards the hand of fate might deal— or so I thought at the time.

Speaking of fate and its mysterious workings, I must relate the second unusual experience that leaves my 12th year forever etched in memory. It was the year that I lost Ichen, my comfort, my anchor, my eternal existence, the secret Self, so secret that I'd about forgotten it lurked within. One waning afternoon while walking home from school, I'm ducking through some neighborhood bushes on a shortcut well traveled by boys like me when, between one footfall and the next, Ichen suddenly vanishes, is inexplicably *gone.* The air of Earth is choked out of my lungs and, gasping for breath, my books fall to the ground in shocking disarray. I'm alone and meager, my soul has shriveled down to usual size, and, for the first time, I'm merely a boy—and I'm afraid, sorely afraid. My foot suspended in air comes abruptly down to earth where the rest of me must now reside.

Wherefore art thou, God? Where hast thou gone?

Sometimes we don't know truth until it vanishes and is beyond reach; I didn't know then that man and God are usually separated by a veil of ignorance. From age 7 to 12 I experienced God as Self, Ichen, even as I could see in the mirror that I was a boy, mostly with a smile on my face, and mostly unafraid. But now, fearful rumination is my soul's activity. I am alone, but I tell no one. I say nothing. As I wrestle with the pain of separation, all I know for certain is that I am different, in ways that I couldn't imagine at the time.

Our family home on Painter Avenue in Whittier, California, featured an attic bedroom on the third floor that, because I was the eldest son, became my very own retreat from all that went on down below. The private bath held a claw-foot bathtub that I adorned with painted flames of yellow and red. Posters, drawings, and art paraphernalia filled empty spaces, and I covered my bed with a salvaged nautical flag of stiff blue canvas to set the artsy mood.

This wonderful retreat had its own outside stairway, an addition that we surmised allowed for a boarder during the Great Depression. The loft was mine now, and I had climbed out of my own depressive state that had been occasioned by the loss of Ichen.

The following summer, I'm sitting at my desk high above the tumult of family life, my loft an isolated sanctuary where anything might happen, but mostly it is where I read books. A reader ever since Ruth Maguire, my fifth-grade teacher, opened the door to magical transport through the written word, I traveled the high seas and, along with the crew, cursed Captain Bligh. I rode with Heinlein to a strange land where I was the stranger, *grokking* it all. I marveled at the angst of Holden Caulfield and wept with Hemingway at the loss of the great fish.

This day finds me drawing, not reading. Fluffy, our longhaired housecat, is lounging on the bed while I sit at my drafting table drawing a picture of my left hand, which is conveniently available for this study. As the drawing progresses I am thinking more about the cat hair on my bedspread than the drawing itself, which I now notice is an excellent one, well done, with forefinger and thumb holding a beaded chain from which dangles a Christian cross. Where did that come from? As I am wondering about this odd appearance on paper of an image that was not consciously intended, a voiced message comes into my head: *You will die at age 33.*

As I stare at the drawing with my mind in some sort of suspended animation, I gradually become aware of Fluffy exiting through the open window and onto the roof. She will then climb down a slender tree to return to Earth, just as I need to do. *What is this?* I think. Like most teenagers, I assumed that I was immortal. This rude announcement that sets my heart racing surely couldn't be coming from my own mind, subconscious or otherwise.

The fear that sends waves of nausea across my internal landscape soon abates. My mind raises a slew of questions that clearly have no answer. I drum my fingers on the drafting table and examine the drawing once again. A cross. Jesus? Is this a Jesus thing? I certainly feel no inclination to get churchy, but do decide to read the New Testament, a vow that soon falls to the wayside in favor of skateboarding and trips to the beach.

I didn't tell my best buddy, Steve Keiser, about this prophetic episode either. He shared my less confounding interests in girls, cars, and rock and roll. Steve and I were typical teenagers of the late '50s, a much less complicated era than those that would shortly follow.

❧

It would be almost 20 years later, in September 1970, that I would have reason to review the subject of personal mortality once again.

Death was an ever-present part of my daily experience at County Hospital. After the first shock of seeing a living person draw a last breath, the soul no longer animating tissue and mind, I didn't give it much thought. The turbulence of life and of love seemed to insulate me from too much thinking about my ever-approaching 33rd year. I wanted insulation from such morbid stuff, and life offered it up without much comment.

I pen a short note to Catherine advising that I'd be working late and would get dinner at the cafeteria, a prospect that brings little anticipatory delight: God-awful food, but the company is generally good. There are a hundred other interns and countless residents who made up the house staff at L.A. County, the largest hospital in the country. Built in the 1920s, it was of federal stone, a monolithic presence sitting high on a hill overlooking the Hispanic barrio from whence many a victim of violence was transported, siren wailing, to its anxious doors.

One of us generally is on hand when an ambulance pulls up, ready to begin the choreographed dance with the devil in an attempt to staunch the flow of life blood and thereby reverse the victim's speedy descent to the netherworld. Throwing a red blanket on the gurney announces to all concerned that the devil has the upper hand. The poor soul is then rushed to the surgical floor without so much as his real name affixed to the big toe—John or Jane Doe until otherwise noted. We are a cadre of hardened souls who, even after a brief time at County, have seen it all. Some of us lose our humanity during this initiation into the brotherhood of healers, and some of us do not, coming out on the other end as physicians of the spirit as well as healers of the body. I count myself in the latter group and am energized and excited about a career in medicine, a huge leap compared to my previous fear of sick people and the hospitals that serve them.

No, I didn't want to be a doctor at all. I signed up to be a dentist, but magical intervention plopped me into my true destiny. And, here I am, an intern at County, dealing with death every day. Sure, there is a dark chord of funereal music playing, but I always, *always* laugh it off.

How did I manage to get here, laughing and crying as human blood seeps into the floor?

Well, college life in the '60s was designed for the likes of me. I loved it. I learned how to drink, how to relate to my social peers, and most of all, how to love. I loved my fraternity brothers. I loved the new vistas that opened with my studies: chemistry, biology, even music appreciation. But most of all, I loved Catherine. I discovered that I was a romantic at heart and I let this devious trait have its way with me. The net result was a great deal of instruction in the ways of the heart, but my grades tumbled in the process.

Then, late one afternoon, I'm sitting alone in Holcomb Gardens listening to the lilting melodies of the carillon bells when an unruly notion seeps into my awareness. *You must be a doctor, not a dentist. You must be...* The message repeats itself. *What is this?* I think as I jump up in alarm. *What is going on?* I stand rooted to the ground for a moment realizing that I'd asked the wrong questions, *Who is this?* being the correct one.

Chapter Three

So Be It

He that would have the fruit must climb the tree.
—Thomas Fuller

February, 1966

Dressed in a pinstriped gray suit, I'm sitting before a panel of somber MDs, each of whom has a copy of my application to Indiana University School of Medicine in front of them. My GPA of 2.7 is a scarlet letter of shame that I wear on my forehead. They can all see it, I know, and I must distract their attention from it. After all, I'd developed great skills of persuasion during my summer vacations spent as a door-to-door encyclopedia salesman.

There is a moment of silence as I formulate my answer to their question. Mentally, I approach the screen door and stick my hand out: *Hi, I'm Dick House and I'd like to tell you about my grand dream of serving mankind as a physician.* I open my satchel and my heart to these folks as the correct notes of an optimistic song grace the air between us, a melody of great promise, great promise indeed.

As is my custom of late, after a hard day's work as a summer construction laborer, selling encyclopedias having lost its appeal, I walk along the lake to the mailbox on McFarland Road. They call me "Doc" at work, and as I hold the letter in my hand at roadside, I fervently hope that the nickname is justified. The cars are whizzing by, the people in them clueless about the dramatic moment that holds me in its icy grip. And then: *You are hereby admitted to the class of 1967 with our hearty congratulations.*

This is one of the sweetest moments of my life, an impossible dream come true. I start sobbing uncontrollably, the letter clutched in my hand, a forever moment of grace as cars whizz by. As I slowly walk back to the house, I stop a moment and reexamine the words, *with our hearty congratulations.* I laugh out loud thinking about the incredible work that it took to get here. No one had been happy about my intended switch to medicine. Girding my loins, a mere year ago I approach Dad with the startling news that I want to be a doctor. He stops sanding the piece of wood and looks up, eyebrows raised. "You want to go to medical school?" He starts blinking his eyes quickly, his outward sign of intensive thought combined with agitation, and after resolving the issue to his internal satisfaction, the eye blinks slow down and he asks, "Can you get in?"

"It's a long shot."

"How long?"

"I have a 2.5."

He smiles and resumes sanding. It isn't merely a long shot, but an impossibility given the rules that govern admission committee deliberations. And yet here it is. I again look to the cloudless blue sky. "So, okay. I'll be a doctor. Is there anything else?" No reply is forthcoming, and I resume walking.

"Okay, captain, sir, God, I believe it now."

Chapter Four

The Fruit of the Vine

I read about the evils of drinking, so I gave up reading.
—Henny Youngman

After the Butler graduation ceremony, on the grassy common not far from Irwin Library, Catherine and I are still capped and gowned, the sun roasting us in our glee. Four years have passed with sandpapery swiftness, leaving us shaped and smooth. The future beckons: for me, medical school; for her, a master's degree.

We walk to the shady expanse beneath a huge oak tree where our four parents greet us with handshakes and hugs. Catherine's mom, also a Catherine, has a worried look on her face, which brings me up short. I'm soon to learn why; the news that is forthcoming casts a sudden pall over our crowd. What spills out of my Catherine's mouth in a torrent of excitement is this: "I've signed a one-year contract to teach dance at Interlochen."

Stunned by this change of plan that until this very moment she's kept to herself, I stare at her in glassy-eyed wonder. My mind leaps into agitated whirring with, *What about our plans to marry?* My mouth, on the other hand, jumps into the uncomfortable silence with a different question. "Where's Interlochen?"

"Near Traverse City, Michigan," she says. "I leave next week." There is general squirming as parents congratulate her and commiserate with my kicked-to-the-curb self.

It is an adept career move for Catherine that I really can't fault. Oblivious to my emotional indigestion, Catherine assures me that she'll be back to finish her master's at Butler and we could hitch-up then—*be patient, you sweet thing.* She plays her cards well that day and wins the hand.

The bench where I'm sitting is on a shady street in the middle of the medical school campus. The dental school is across Michigan Avenue, where Steve Keiser has been studying for a year, having gained an early entry as a result of stellar grades at Butler. I'm a bit jealous, I admit. I'm also jealous of the medical students that hurry by attired in short white coats with "Dr. So-and-So" embossed on plastic nametags. Their white conductive safety shoes that dissipate static electricity are required in the OR and also serve to announce to all, *I am on my way to serve humanity.*

Classes don't start for a few weeks and yesterday was my last day at the construction job. "See ya, Doc. Good luck." I actually had to wipe away a tear. I loved those guys and the rough and ready life they lived.

The next day I walk into the ER at University Hospital wearing a white coat, white conductive shoes, and a smile. The waiting room is packed even at this hour, the smell of illness and rubbing alcohol thickening the air. I brush through the door to the treatment area and approach an intern writing notes on a chart. I peek at his nametag. "Dr. Swartz, I'm a medical student and would like to help out." With the briefest glance, he nods. "Ever sew up a laceration?" he asks, as he continues to write.

"Uh, no."

"Meet me in room three."

With the barest of instruction I learn how to inject Xylocaine, wash a wound, and sew it up using instrument-tie stitching. The result is quite satisfactory: my first patient contact with tens of thousands to follow, and it goes very well. I am so elated that I barely remember the rest of that shift in the ER. It is this sort of elation combined with exhaustion that would follow me all through my medical training. I had found my place, my promised destiny that had been prescribed (by whom, God?) as a tonic against a vale of darkness that seemed to be lurking deep within my persona. No matter; *just get on with it.*

The smell is the first assault on my senses. It is of formalin, a complex chemical smell that begins softly in my nose and then gradually increases in intensity until the olfactory center in my suddenly awakened brain registers a *piercing smell* that makes me gasp in astonishment—awful.

The second assault is visual. I'm standing in the entry area of a warehouse-sized room near two circular, white-tiled hand-washing stations. *I could puke there if it comes to that,* my mind volunteers. My eyes then make the effort to look beyond these stark white stations to rows and rows of stainless steel humidors, each the size and shape of a coffin, each raised up on steel legs to waist-high convenience, and all of them closed up, thank God.

The third assault is auditory. Malcolm Herring, Dan Heller, and I are among a clustered group of students nervously chattering in the hallway when the professor unlocks the door to the anatomy lab and we nervously walk in. The abrupt *silence* is shocking. Instead of human conversation, all I hear is death not speaking. *Maybe I'm too sensitive for all this*, I think. *I hate what my senses are reporting and don't want to be here. My toes curl up in my shoes and want to run me out of the room, out of Indiana, but where? Where do I go? Aha, Laguna Beach—Shaw's Cove. My toes relax as I go there.*

There are 22 steps going down to the beach that gradually take me from the world of worries to that of inner peace. The stairway is bordered by two rusted handrails that are blistered and damp to my touch. Wild nasturtiums line the ravine on both sides, the orange flowers and greenery glistening with dew. Eucalyptus boughs shade my gradual barefoot descent into grace, step by step. The fragrance soon gradually shifts from the gummy perfume of the Australian trees to whiffs of seaweed and salt air. The cave-like arbor with stairs is dark enough to generate a bright glare at its opening on the hot sand, a white light that reflexively throws my hand up to shade my blinking eyes.

What a brilliant sight. The crashing waves send spray over dark rocks pockmarked with shallow pools of sea water and sea life. The sun sends reflected beams that scatter into a thousand dancing pinpoints of light. The ocean breeze takes tufts of foam and blows them to and fro. It is a sheltered cove with steep cliffs all around, ice plants growing down them with flowers of pink and puce. The beach is of white sand, dark mounds of sculpted ocean, rocks rising here and there. The blue-green sea and frothy waves crash in crescendo and retreat in the endless rhythm of primal life, where it all began.

Malcolm and I look at each other, our eyes flashing thoughts that we share silently. We start walking toward our assigned humidor as Dan follows behind us. It is he that opens it, exposing tissue and bone that is organized into humanness: Bessie, an old woman long dead and smelling of formalin. There is no grace here, no life, no nothing at all but a remnant that Bessie's mind ordered around once upon a time; her life a mystery to us, her death a great mystery as well.

Death.

Birth.

Life.

These things rise up from Bessie and slap me in the face. My mind shudders, its ignorance palpable, tasting of dry spit and formalin. Wrenching myself back from Shaw's Cove to the unpleasant present, I stare at lifeless Bessie as the drone of the professor's voice drowns out the sounds of sand and water. My hand trembles as I make an incision in her blue-white skin.

A thousand times, Malcolm, Dan, and I stand before Bessie. Sometimes the sun shines through the bank of windows on the eastern wall, and many times it is the harsh fluorescent light above the humidor that hums away the darkness of night as we discover Bessie's secrets, the ticking clock on the white tiled wall our metronome.

All medical students in America experience this initiation into the grossness of human anatomy. A few run out of the room, but mostly they return. The experience *needs* to be unpleasant, as one's own comfort zone is sacrificed to higher purpose. This is an apt summary of what transpires throughout the course of four years: expansion of self. This medical *initiation* grants personal authority to allow well-meaning interference in the lives of others: do this, don't do that, take this, eat that. Subverting this process by making it less difficult weakens the system in its entirety and perhaps robs the practitioner of his greatest tool, the power of healing.

Biochemistry, pathology, human physiology, and gross anatomy are all first-year courses, each of which requires full-time study. The impossibility of attending to this dilemma is a problem that each of us solves differently, based on personal inclination and talent brought to the task. I solve it by spending most of my off-time at Butler's Irwin Library in adrenalin-fueled study that I counter each evening with a dose of red wine. My entire universe devolves to these quadrants: class, study, wine, and bed. It is a semi-workable system that finds me in the clutches of an addictive demon even as I excel in medical studies.

One winter morning at dawn, I'm sitting behind Dick McVay as he drives us three to the medical school, and as we are crossing over the White River Bridge, I have my left hand on the window crank, ready to roll it down quickly should my gorge rise in protest to the red wine I drank last night. I always have hangovers—every nasty morning. Always nausea, and, increasingly, self-contempt. I see the back of Dick's head as he warbles out "Hey Jude," singing along with The Beatles on the radio at this ungodly hour. My mind then takes an abrupt turn to the beetles that seem to be eating up my guts.

I can't take it anymore. I pray to God, if there be one, to help me get through this morning's agony. What to do?

That day I use a campus phone to make an appointment with Dr. Silverman, the school psychiatrist, who is able to see me that very afternoon. Of course, I am feeling much better by then, the emergent nature of my problem having receded a great deal. I turn on my charm as I sit across from this kindly man.

"So," I conclude, after telling a rehearsed tale of the red-wine blues, "What should I do?"

This man of few words leans forward, elbows on desk, and looks at me intently. "Stop drinking."

Aghast, I pull my chair back a bit, mouth dropping open. It is then that I realize that what I really want is a good hangover remedy, not interference in my well-crafted, four-quadrant program of life. I nod and exit stage left, the little devil on my left shoulder rolling around in fits of laughter. Ho ho ho, ha ha.

I've been summoned! A year has passed and winter again has set its frost upon the cornfields and bare trees, a land of exquisite beauty that even I, an overburdened student of human mechanics, can appreciate.

Catherine would like me to visit Interlochen if I can find the time, her voice a reminder that I have sludged up my heart with the unimportant exigencies of daily endeavor. "Of course; I'll be there Saturday." There is a smallish red flag that my mind conjures up: *Why now?* She was soon to finish up her work at Interlochen and return to Butler. *Maybe she's finally lonely*, I think. I certainly am. My loneliness has grown to gigantic proportions even though I am with people all day and a goodly part of the night as well. It's the sort of empty longing that is chilling and desperate, best hidden by a smile and hearty laugh, one clown face painted in white with a grin and the other fashioned into a frown with blue greasepaint and tears.

After my exhausting moonlighting shift at St. Vincent's is finally over, I jump into the little red MG that is my daily transport. The recent snowfall makes driving dicey and, admittedly, my little English sports car was not a thoughtful purchase. But I love the damn thing, and even though it doesn't have a heater or snow tires, somehow I make it to Michigan several long, cold hours later.

Catherine is standing outside her small bungalow smoking a cigarette when I finally pull up. Her face is shrouded in the shadow of the overhanging eves, but my heart leaps in excited anticipation as I slide to a stop in the icy muck. The tall pine trees that are everywhere are hung with melting snow and the sun is dazzling as I unfold out of the little car. Catherine steps out into the sunlight and douses her cigarette. I see trouble in her face; her graceful dancer movements have been stage-crafted into clumsy jerks. She's been crying. No romantic rejoining of hearts here. *What hath come to pass? What noble enterprise hath been rent asunder?* I'm now in a Shakespearean tragedy, I think, as our pitiable embrace confirms the worst.

Inside her small bungalow it is too warm for comfort as we sit facing one another, each on a twin bed. She looks at me with questioning eyes but says nothing about my waxed handlebar mustache, new to her. She doesn't care about such things, her upset far too great to accommodate anything but her own image that I reflect back to her. She sobs and gushes out her lines, which my astonished mind reviews with wonder: *There is a new player in our drama. Enter stage right, Robert, playing a lively trumpet concerto—or is it a Handel funeral dirge?*

"It just happened," says Catherine, the love of my life. "We were lonely and started sleeping together," she adds as she grasps a short dagger of shiny steel and plunges it into my beating heart. The icy steel sends spurts of adrenalin into my bloodstream that make me jump to my feet and clutch my chest. My eyes scan the small room, taking in the poster of Nureyev leaping in midair. Would that I were he, gracious God. Would that I were he.

I am never the same after that, but Catherine continues being Catherine. As I quickly thumb through the script once again, I can't find an exit for either of us. We are bound into this tragedy with the sound of a trumpet concerto fading away, then silence.

This is where I miss a cue. I should have up and left, stage right. *Adios, my dear.* Instead I bundle up all my hurt, stuff it down deep, and forgive her.

The Red Carpet, a quiet bar by day, transforms itself into a raucous inn by night, the tavern keeper and his flouncy wenches sloshing us students with beer and ribald suggestions filled with impropriety. Weekends, Dirty George holds sway, playing the piano and telling his hilarious jokes which are liberally laced with "fuck"s and other profane English words. He helps sell beer and provides a lusty release from daytime worries. *Laugh, and laugh hysterically, you all; drink up.* Malcolm, Dan, and I are weekend regulars, but my roomies, to their credit, have more sober entertainments in mind.

The fact that they tolerate my various excesses is testimony to their good nature and perhaps my good luck. We all get along.

One memorable night, I find myself sitting at the curved bar on my favorite barstool as Dirty George is in fine form, his jokes filling the air with laughter. Before leaving for his break, he turns on some radio rock-and-roll: the Grateful Dead? I drain the last of six beers and am thinking about a trip to the john when I notice the bassline growing in intensity. The drumbeats mixed with bass guitar are starting to *propel* me up toward the black-painted ceiling. I float. The ceiling is the night sky and the sounds are humming into my heart's circulation. My body is, for the first time, filled with bliss and not pain.

The bassline fades and, upon fading, floats me down to the barstool of human existence, where my companions have not noticed my absence. I stagger home on foot since my little red car is also drunk.

As a third-year medical student, I discover that I am really good at being a doctor. No more classroom tedium and no more worries about making the grade; I am in my element working one on one with patients who listen as I sing my song of health and good living. I in turn listen to Sergeant Pepper's magical band and continue to go *one toke over the line* as we celebrate with the streaming colors of Peter Max flying overhead.

Catherine and I, now married, move into the Pumpkin, so named because of its orange-painted clapboard and yellow trim. It is an old Victorian on New Jersey Avenue and 13th Street in the heart of the black section of Indianapolis. Larry, an enterprising psych resident, and his wife, Vivian, had bought two such homes side by side and spent time and money on restoring them to reasonable functionality. We happily move into one of them as I assemble a crew of prospective tenants to live there as well. We painted the Pumpkin orange to shine brightly in the darkness of the rat-infested ghetto. It is a dangerous game that challenges prudence and probity, a '60s dream inserted into the squalid nightmare of race relations and social deterioration, but it works.

I knock on neighborhood doors, suspicious peeks through curtains and screen-door conversations eventually establishing a white man's treaty: no violence in return for free medical advice and treatment of minor ailments—spread the word. Yes, there is still gunfire in the night and roaming packs of rats next door, but our orange and yellow oasis is mostly left undisturbed. Our living situation is not to Catherine's liking, and for this I accept the blame, my pseudo-hippie imaginings in 1969 being a longed-for simulacrum of freedom—a distant reflection of Ken Kesey's merry pranksters as they proclaimed free love and acid revelations, traveling across the country in a flashing neon bus.

Years later during a nostalgic return to this fair city, I have occasion to drive down New Jersey Avenue, now paved and well landscaped, the two Victorians still standing proudly, the orange and yellow paint covered up with gray gentility, as is the entire neighborhood. I hope that our efforts in 1969 had something to do with this transition—the rats and poverty no doubt moved on.

I am neither a hippie nor a merry prankster; I am a young doctor about to complete his schooling. What now?

My uncle, Howard House, always a twinkle in his eye, founded the Otologic Medical Group in Los Angeles in 1959. I remember the grand opening when I was a teenager, with celebrities and gentle folk, the elite of the city, drinking champagne and eating shrimp cocktails while slapping Howard on the back and swapping the jokes that were ever his delight.

His brother, Bill House, was also a visionary whose great energy and imagination brought about new surgical approaches for hearing-related disorders—many of them still in use today. These great men were secret role models for me, unearthed and recognized as such during my medical years. Could I join the clinic? Is this my medical destiny, or have I been too lax, too earthy, and too diligent in the pursuit of Bacchus?

Brushing aside these concerns, I take an elective course in the microsurgery of the ear. Peering through the observer tube that was invented by Bill, I watch a local otologist, Dr. Bill Wright, as he performs surgeries pioneered by Howard years before. Yes, this is what I want; the micro-world of auditory conduction that brings speech and music back to awareness. This is where I belong. The intensity of this ambition becomes my northern star.

Degrees in hand, Catherine and I pack our few worldly goods into the miniscule back seat of my red Porsche 912. She is in a foul mood and broods in silence even as I hum the remembered notes and whisper the memorized lyrics of my favorite tune from the musical *The Roar of the Greasepaint—The Smell of the Crowd*: "There is a beautiful land where all your dreams come true..."

Indiana passes quickly, our lives left behind amid rows of freshly planted corn and drizzly rain. There is an urgency that pushes the Porsche along at high speed as I watch out for cops. The L.A. County Hospital wants me on the wards four days hence—four travel days of punctuation between one life and the next. The gigantic arch of St. Louis looms as Catherine finds her voice, which has been engaged by rising spirits. "Where is Palmdale?" she asks.

"It's over the foothills from L.A., out in the desert," I reply.

"I guess we'll need another car."

I nod and assure her that this need has not escaped my notice: a BMW?

Catherine has secured a position as instructor in modern dance at California Institute of the Arts, a distant runner-up to her long-held dream of a New York City dance company, and is just now, as we approach Tulsa, Oklahoma, deciding that it is worthy of at least some enthusiasm.

Why do I love this woman who is so difficult to love? I don't know, and don't think about it often for fear that close examination will reveal some flaw in my operating system that will shut down the entire works.

As behind schedule as we are, I pull off the freeway at La Jolla, California, and heed the alluring call of the sea. Catherine, who doesn't understand, remains in the car as I walk down the slick concrete steps near Bird Rock, the roar of ocean waves amplified by the rolling black stones on shore. Standing in awe, a thought comes forth unbidden. *I am here, too, and always have been. I am everywhere.* This Voice speaks to my encumbered heart and I listen.

July, 1972

Internship now over and done with, the first year of ENT residency is actually a full year of general surgery. Rich Clark and I are assigned to Good Samaritan Hospital in downtown L.A., a gentleman doctor's enclave where the rich and famous appear on the wards, not the down-and-out of our County experience.

Dr. Michelson, our new boss, is larger than life, the best general and vascular surgeon on staff. If John Wayne had played a doctor, Dr. Mike would have been a good role model, with his unfiltered camel cigarettes, whiskey after sundown, and unassailable confident swagger; a man of few words and big deeds. We soon love the guy and work damn hard for him, we, his sidekicks at Good Sam.

Rich Clark, thin and balding, his pale complexion ever ready to flush with emotion, is, like so many of my close friends, cheerful and optimistic, ready to smother problems with multiple solutions and hard work. Moreover, he fancies himself an artist, as do I. We share a nice call room with real amenities including a window with a view of pine trees that are often noisy with blue jays. We set up easels and stock the refrigerator with beer and vodka to fuel our creative impulses after call hours have passed. Why not? Rich and I soon have a room full of drawings and paintings that we eventually hang at a Pasadena gallery, even selling one or two.

Work with Dr. Mike and other surgeons on staff is exhilarating, the art of medicine coming forward as well as lessons in surgical technique. We not only assist in the OR, but we also interview patients beforehand and change their dressings afterward. Bedside manner, that elusive quality that defines a good doctor, was not an issue at the County, but is very important at Good Sam. We cultivate it, learning medical diplomacy and good manners along the way. Rich Clark not only shines his star at Good Sam, he ends up as an ENT surgeon on staff there after finishing his residency.

Steve Keiser finds his perfect spot in Santa Ana near Disneyland, his dental practice already thriving. I take our new BMW out for a drive and it decides to take me to Steve's place for an impromptu visit. He has not yet met Paula, the love of his life, nor has he started restoring vintage cars, the other love of his life. We throw back a few beers and relive some of our golden moments, two best friends separated by distance and proclivities, our fraternal bond forever intact.

The year passes quickly, the memory of Good Sam soon overpowered by the avalanche of gunshot wounds and general mayhem that enlivens L.A. County Hospital. Sleepless nights and demanding days leave little room for art. What I discover in its place is the beauty of microsurgery, which holds me in thrall. I am not only good at it, but fast, a God-given talent that surprises even me. The idea of joining my family's clinic seems operational, but there looms a disquieting problem: Catherine and I are frequently at odds and, dare I say it, my friend Jack Daniels, a lower companion, urges me to give up this dream on his behalf. He is a demanding fellow, that Jack.

Catherine has taken to her bed in a black depression that has gone on for days. The clinic secretary comes hurrying over to my workstation at County where I am examining a patient who has episodic vertigo. The message she whispers makes my head spin in vertiginous alarm: "Your wife has taken a full bottle of sleeping pills. She just called and sounds awful."

I spin out of County and race home to our apartment in Alhambra. I could never be sure. I couldn't be certain—this time it might be the real thing.

There is silence in the apartment, a bad sign. I tiptoe in, careful to be quiet, and then flip open the bedroom door. Catherine is alive, but not well. She's rumpled and clearly distraught, sending daggers of upset my way; the TV is on at low volume. It is not a scene of impending disaster, but of a chronic, disastrous mal-union of two well-meaning souls.

We are done, this I know. I do not have the courage to end it, but it soon ends itself.

The desperate night that she left, she ensured her exit, stage left, by slashing my paintings that hung on the wall. It took this brilliant piece of stagecraft to suitably arouse my ire. I yelled, I screamed; she got out, suitcase and my heart in hand.

The next morning, I awoke on the kitchen floor, a turd of the earth, smelling of shit and alcohol. I was two hours late, missed rounds, missed my morning clinic, missed it all. God, what agony.

♠

The *Who am I?* part of the question is moot. *Where am I?* becomes an issue. I come to my senses the next day sitting at the counter of the Pasadena Big Boy Restaurant: *a fugue state to preserve sanity*, I was later told. The precariousness of my perch hits me as I drink black coffee. I discover that I've misplaced my car, a vintage 356 Porsche, white with red interior. I consider asking the police to help me find it...not a good idea, not a good idea at all. Out on Colorado Boulevard, the crisp winter air seeps into my blackness and I walk about, one foot following the other, one breath at a time. I marvel at the people walking toward me on the sidewalk; some even say hello. They are normal, I think, and blissfully unaware.

There it is, my car, on Los Robles Avenue, patiently awaiting its driver whose mind has been saved, but whose heart has gone missing.

♠

The last time I see Catherine, she is living with two gay men in the San Fernando Valley, much closer to Cal-Arts.

"You look great," I say, knowing that this would please her. She smiles.

"So do you," she replies, both of us understanding that this small lie is a good thing between us. We had been married for a difficult six years.

We embrace for a last time and I jump into my Porsche and head for the freeway. In my rearview mirror I see her standing next to her blue BMW, but she doesn't wave.

Chapter Five

The Bradbury Rewire

Psychoanalysis is in essence a cure through love.
—Sigmund Freud

"Hello, Ken? This is your cousin, Dick. I need some help." My hand trembles and quick sobs are impossible to hold back. Ken, a classically trained psychiatrist, calls me back in a few minutes. "You have an appointment with Dr. Kline today at 3 o'clock," he tells me. "He's the chair of the department at USC."

On the outside, the Bradbury Building where I'm to meet Dr. Kline looks like any other brown brick structure of the late 1800s scattered around Los Angeles. It is on the inside where transport occurs, where imagination soars like the five-story atrium the building boasts, the glass ceiling admitting natural sunlight to bathe all who enter. Polished wood gleams on banisters supported by black cast-iron balusters, the stair steps of Belgian marble worn down by a thousand footsteps. With complex emotions, I mount these steps with resolve overcoming resistance.

The small anteroom so common to psychiatric practice is devoid of warmth; a place for magazines to grow old and anxiety to rise. I'm always early, always anxious, and this fact is broadcast by my sweaty hands. Must I shake when we meet? The handshake issue is so troubling that I consider leaving, hands on the armrests, ready to bolt. The door springs open and a well-groomed matron, eyes straight ahead, passes through the small room and leaves. I'm flummoxed; what to do? I stare at the door and it opens again. Dr. Frank Kline, MD, peers out. He is tall and thin, a fringe of gray hair puffing above his ears, a half smile to complement his half-glasses over which he studies me for a moment.

Sometimes we know things that are unknowable. As he says hello with a caring voice, I begin to sob, the kind of sobs that are unstoppable, wet, and gut wrenching. A part of my mind wonders at the incredible freedom that I feel, the release.

He waves me in and I plop down in his office with a box of supplied Kleenex. We don't shake hands—a small relief. I apologize for my lack of grace and soon stop sniveling.

"Well," he says. "Ken says you've recently split from your wife." His choice of words couldn't be more accurate: I feel split and halved like a piece of overripe fruit.

I nod, my throat still immobilized by cataracts of sadness. *Why am I so distraught?*

Sigmund Freud developed a set of fairly workable theories about the subconscious—a hidden valley of emotional determinants that can lead to surprising dysfunction in day-to-day life. Distant dad, overprotecting mom, sexual urges that titillate and overpower reason—these all swim in the seas of the subconscious, waiting to explode into painful manifestation when one least expects it. The basic premise of Freudian analysis is that identifying these subconscious imprints will extinguish their power in a blaze of light. The agent of this process is the analyst who becomes a benign father figure and has the best interests of the patient at heart. The transference of authority from real dad to stand-in dad takes a while (thus my subsequent weekly appointments), but for how many years? How many boxes of Kleenex will it take?

Of course, as I sit across from Dr. Frank Kline the first few times, I have little awareness of these things, but I know without a doubt that I am in the right place with the right guy.

The initial session leaves me drained but far more comfortable. I shake Dr. Kline's hand upon leaving, and, to my surprise, my hand is dry and cool. As I pass through the anteroom, there is another well-groomed matron thumbing nervously through a dog-eared magazine. *How many of us are there?* I wonder—the walking wounded of L.A.

Dr. Crabtree, the head of otologic surgery at County, is visibly angry. Not a good thing. I have been called into his office for a rare sit-down meeting and know exactly what is coming. I start singing a tune from *The Fantasticks* in my head as the sweat starts pooling in my crevices. *Soon it's gonna rain, I can feel it, soon it's gonna rain, rain like hell...*

"I don't care what is going on in your personal life," he says, as I began nodding. "You will not show up late for surgery with alcohol on your breath." He pauses and turns even redder of face. The unmentioned fact that I am a potential candidate for training and a career at my family's clinic makes the whole thing worse. James Crabtree is a partner at the Otologic Medical Group (OMG), he is one of the world's best otologic surgeons, and he is furious. There is little doubt in my mind that Bill and Howard would soon hear about my felonious behavior. Kaput, done, finished.

After this stormy session and my vow to reform, I shoot into the men's room to cool down. In the mirror I stare at the riverboat gambler with the sagging handlebar. This is a huge bet gone sour indeed.

The next afternoon, we are presenting otologic cases to Dr. James Sheehy, also a world-class ear surgeon at the OMG. I can tell that he has heard of my fall from grace, but instead of anger, he responds with kindness, a fact that I will never forget. God bless you, Dr. Sheehy.

Every Thursday afternoon, I park on Third Street with a generous tip to the attendant. The vast City Market, across from the Bradbury Building, features fresh local vegetables, fruit, seafood, Mexican fast food, beer, wine, sweet juice coolers, and all manner of edible stuff. As it's not far from Fifth Street's skid row, the homeless, destitute, and mentally disturbed are evident everywhere. *These people,* I think, *are my fellows.* Sure, I drive a nice car and have plenty of money, and when I work at the jail, I'm free to go home after my shift. I have choices that these people do not, but my choices have landed me here on Third Street too. Even worse, most of my Third Street companions look happier than I am.

Every Thursday afternoon at 2:55 p.m. I sit on a barstool at City Market and toss back a shot of sweet wine before walking across the street and up three flights to explore the depths of my psyche, much like my dumpster-diving friends down below begin their search for their daily sustenance, one shot of port at a time.

Dr. Kline gradually morphs into my stand-in father, just as Dr. Freud imagined he would. This kind man becomes my authoritative confidant, my anchor in life who allows me to transcend the murky determinants I had unconsciously acquired during child-hood and adolescence, or perhaps even before. My new dad gives me a leg-up, and, miraculously, I get better, and my life starts becoming easier to live.

Dr. Kline doesn't have to prescribe a remedy for my broken heart. I already know what would fix it: It is the power of new love that does the mending of the heart. I start looking, ready to love once again. My first date is a beautiful young woman whom I'll call Janice, a nurse at Children's Hospital. After my shift on pediatrics, we meet in the parking garage, where she retrieves a flask of whisky from under her car seat, and we sit looking at other cars and the people who drive them away. We get very drunk and she confesses her battle with anorexia—and alcohol—and suggests a lay in the backseat. My heart is not at all happy, nor is it mending. I climb out of the small car and say goodbye to Janice, who is mad as hell, her words creating an echoing fusillade of parking garage invective.

I find that romantic love is as elusive as a winning lottery ticket.

Who is she?

I feel a certain restlessness that demands *adventure*. I show up at Laidlaw Harley Davidson one Saturday and say as much to the salesman, Big Mike. "Well, sir," he replies with enthusiasm, "I have just the ticket to ride: a 1,000-cc Sportster." And ride it I did, the loud, shiny thing of black and chrome becoming my chariot of transport as I roar out of the dealership and into the world at large.

Now, where is she?

Even though my initial efforts at finding true love were dismal failures of one sort or another, Dr. Kline encourages me to keep looking. Our weekly sessions find me regaining composure. I discover that I could get along with less self-medicating and awaken each morning with increasing optimism, carrying no alcohol fumes to work.

I love surgery. I spend as much time in the OR as possible doing all sorts of procedures from tonsillectomies—in five minutes, mind you—to complicated ear surgeries with one of the OMG doctors in attendance. My star rises, but nothing erases the blemish of emotional breakdown completely. Nonetheless, I am increasingly restored to good standing in the eyes of our residency director, Dr. Clay Whitaker, an important fellow as it turns out.

Every morning after rounds, Dr. Whitaker convenes an informal discussion group for senior residents at a table in the cafeteria. The topics for discussion range from world affairs to local politics, about which he holds definite opinions. I am among those who curry his favor—for the obvious reason that he holds our post-residency futures in his hands. His recommendation could make or break.

It is hard for me to imagine that I'd soon be a real, honest-to-God practicing doctor after all these years. It's time to do more than imagine. I put out feelers at the OMG with half-hearted enthusiasm. Not only are my prospects considerably dimmed, but the commitment required is daunting. World-class doctors don't have time to sit idly at the beach or pursue art as a serious hobby—or get blasted on weekends. World-class otologic surgeons don't look like riverboat gamblers and ride Harleys. They just don't. It is a no-go, the dream shattered, destiny's hammer at work; my inquiries at the OMG are gently rebuffed.

Dr. Whitaker and I are the only ones lingering over cups of coffee one Monday morning, the others gone off to the wards.

"Say, Dick," he says with a wrinkled brow. "Jim DeGrazio over in San Gabriel is looking for a young associate. Interested?"

"What kind of practice?" I ask, trying to leave eagerness out of my voice.

"General ENT; he doesn't do much ear work, but he trained here at County."

The fact that this offer is on the table as we sit in the noisy cafeteria means that Dr. DeGrazio knows all about my particulars and is okay with the package. Clay Whitaker often acts as our medical matchmaker and has had years of experience negotiating informal contracts for graduating residents; most matches work out.

"Thanks, Dr. Whitaker," I say. "Of course I'm interested." I called Dr. DeGrazio and, at some point during the conversation, he became Jim and he started calling me Richard.

The town of San Gabriel takes its name from the California mission that was established by Junipero Serra in the 18th century. A Franciscan monk, he had a knack for locating early missions in choice locations with enduring utility in the years that followed. The California wine industry owes its beginnings to vines planted at the San Gabriel Mission, and, of more immediate importance, it is where Dr. DeGrazio's office is located.

As I walk up the stairs to his office suite, I wonder at the tales I've heard: good doctor, good surgeon, strong family man, but watch out. He's got an Italian temper; don't cross him. He stands up behind his desk, extending his hand across it. I take in his head mirror, the archaic badge of our specialty, and shake his hand vigorously. Jim is shorter than I, dark hair going bald, a winsome smile and crinkles around his dark eyes. I love the guy instantly.

"Sit," he says, and I do for the next hour that stretches into two. His wife, Arlene, calls to remind him that he's late for dinner.

Jim and I get along famously, although we are more like distant cousins than brothers. He is tidy and conservative, a good businessman, and I, the toned-down eccentric, no handlebar at this point, but a full beard and a long plait of hair that I wore in a queue. The odd couple, as it were, contemplating partnership.

One Thursday afternoon in late summer it is raining in downtown L.A., an unusual event, as most rain falls in the winter months. There is a broken crate of oranges on the sidewalk in front of City Market, which has attracted the attention of several scavengers. One such soul is a regular at the jail where I still pulled weekend shifts. A Hispanic man, he has a florid complexion tinged with the gray look of chronic grime unspoiled by tears or soap. *Why is this man laughing? How can he eat the unpeeled orange with such gusto?* I want to know these simple things.

Somehow I understand that the brown brick building across the street is to be the pathway for answers. I sprint through the traffic and rain and walk up the stairs to the fourth floor, where I find that the office door is locked. I twist the knob a few times and look at my watch: 3 p.m. on the dot. *Has he forgotten me?*

Alarmed, my heart starts to race as true panic sets in, my brow and hands perspiring. I wait a moment, take a few deep breaths and start walking back down the stairs, head bowed in frustrated sadness.

"Richard?" calls Dr. Frank Kline, as I reach the third floor. "Over here; you were on the wrong floor."

Chapter Six

The Sandy Beach of Love

Love doesn't make the world go 'round. Love
is what makes the ride worthwhile.
—Franklin P. Jones

May, 1976

It has been a busy night at the jail with little sleep possible. The full moon? Mike is in a particularly irascible mood and is giving the officers a hard time as they bring their charges into the dispensary. Mike keeps a flask in his desk drawer and has been hitting it a little too often, perhaps because we have worked together for three long years, and this is my last shift at Parker Center. It's time to move on. At precisely 7 a.m., I gather my few things and stick out my hand. No hugs are in the offing; we are too close for that.

"Seeya, Mike."

"Good luck, Doc."

I wipe away a tear and buzz my way out. I'm glad to be done with it, I suppose, but I'll miss the clatter and noise of it all—and the Hollenbeck burrito from El Tepiac in the barrio. The indigestion that comes with it helps me stay awake during the melee of night work. And I'll miss Mike, the little Irishman who always has my back.

As I walk out into the brisk morning air with clouds now showing color, there are several women standing outside waiting to retrieve their wayward husbands who have spent the night in the tank. I wave to them as the curtain comes down and I exit stage right.

It is Saturday, and with my residency work at County all but done, I feel a true sense of freedom as I drive the Santa Monica freeway to the beach. I have a jug of Tom Collins mix laced with vodka to help set the mood and am soon lazing in the noonday sun watching waves and pretty girls as both come and go in an intoxicating beach rhythm.

The crashing waves that creep ever closer to me as the tide comes in become magical, slow-motion drum riffs that soon have me feeling the essence of something far deeper than ocean and sand, an elemental *force* that commands and orchestrates everything. It is for these moments that I draw breath—as brief and infrequent as they may be. The exquisite moment soon fades to the ordinary, a loss of precious endearment, a loss of wholeness that leaves me scattered again like the infinite grains of sand that I slowly sift through my fingers.

I get up awkwardly and walk across the hot expanse of sand to the public restrooms of cinderblock and concrete. As I enter, there is a flash of darkness and a smell of loathing that seeps upward from the wet concrete and into my feet; a slimy feel of evil. My breath comes in gasps as I shudder at the urinal. *Hurry, Richard, get out of this hellish place,* the Voice says. My mind is greatly disturbed by this unexpected thing, this burst of intrusive and unexpected evil. I can't sit on my beach towel now. Instead, I walk along the shore, my left ear attuned to the sound of breaking waves and my eyes looking ahead for some form of beauty, some atonement for this touch of slime.

It takes time, but the ocean is forgiving of all sins and is vastly bigger than any evil thing. As I walk, I do see beauty and my spirits lift as I laugh at myself and my unruly imagination. I walk.

I see her, finally and at last, sitting on a beach towel, reading something. As I turn and approach, I see that she's reading a pamphlet on vertigo, of all things. She sees my shadow and looks up. Brown eyes, frizzy sun-bleached hair, and a half smile. Very thin and sexy, too. I love her. *I love this one.* I experience such joy in the feeling of this love. I don't know her name; she hasn't said a word; perhaps she's married...it doesn't matter—at all. Nothing that I feel is dependent on her. It is an aura of freedom that I feel, a pure *knowing* that is independent of her thoughts and actions.

"Do you have vertigo?" I ask. I didn't even have to think of what to say; it was all laid out for me.

"Yes, it comes and goes."

"I treat vertigo all the time," I say, somewhat lamely. She shades her eyes with her hand and looks up at me more carefully. I don't look like a doctor, after all. "May I sit?" She smiles and nods.

Slim, whose given name is Peggy, lives a few blocks from where we are sitting on the sand. She works in a T-shirt factory but is a member of Mensa, a smart lass who sees no need to pursue ambition. She lives simply and fully; her apartment, I soon discover, is full of plants; 50 or so. She lives in a verdant jungle and is, as I've come to suspect, the incarnation of my longing.

We walk to her apartment and begin to love.

Unlike Catherine, Slim is always upbeat and fun. She, a people person, has many friends and loves to party. I find myself being tugged out of my neurotic shell and actually like being peopled up.

What began as two hearts united becomes an expanded universe of interaction with like-minded people, dinners out, parties, dancing, fun, and plenty of cannabis-fueled sex. I am reanimated as my blistered heart not only heals, but starts running the show.

We move into a modest home in Alhambra, and moving day is mostly about plant relocation in various sun-favored areas of the house. The landlord encourages our painting and landscaping efforts, both new to me, as Slim and I build a colorful life together, the ride really worthwhile at last.

We are married on the beach in Malibu in front of Ken and Joan's house, the Moody Blues singing from speakers on the sand. There are dolphins far out to sea that listen and watch. I imagine faint applause from the heavens...too much grass, perhaps. Just before the ceremony, Slim and I light up a Thai stick, which expands our perception into the blue-green realms of spinning wheels and flashing lights. That, and the champagne, has me floating in the beyond, where memory is not etched but dwells only in the present.

I snap back into this reality as the plane lands in Tahiti, an unreal island of exquisite beauty laden with fruity smells and drippy air. A speedboat ride later has we merry travelers riding in an open-sided bus winding through the tropical jungle of nearby Moorea. Colorful parrots and black myna birds squawk and sing their simple songs in the lush canopy overhead.

Passing through the gates of Club Med, we disembark and are soon clustered in excited groups—rum drinks for everyone in the welcome pavilion where a French clown claps for our attention.

"Bonjour!"

Our clown then says a few words in French for those who are fellow countrymen, laughs and guffaws the result. In English, he wishes us a pleasant two weeks, but, "Watch out for the fish, the stonefish, that kills you in 10 minutes." His earnest look belies any frivolity; he is serious. "These fish have spines of poison, not to step on him." With that, he dances around and then does a cartwheel as our crowd is gradually dispersed, guides leading us to our thatched huts and the unbelievable beauty that surrounds them.

I later find out that the clown is a French doctor who carries an antidote for stonefish venom in a pouch on his belt.

After two weeks of tropical sun, we are tan and languid. Our new Canadian friends, John and Anne, make up our laughing foursome and become favored travel partners as we rendezvous in other beautiful spots on Earth in the years that follow.

It is a magical time of sex and sun, love and laughter, our hearts melded into a destined union.

I did see an ugly stonefish hidden in the colorful coral, but didn't step on him.

After a year of practice with Jim DeGrazio, I become a full partner—I wear three-piece suits and develop a great reputation at the hospital for fast, clean work in the OR. Slim and I buy a house in the Sierra Madre foothills that is perfect for entertaining. There is a deck overlooking the shaded backyard and a furnished guest house with a red tile roof and white stucco walls, a red bougainvillea growing up the wall near the shaded entry.

The wooden deck generates my moments of peace. It is my new oceanic retreat where wind-tousled trees take the place of sea, salt, and sand.

I seem to need more and more deck time as work pressures and night call take their toll. Slim doesn't like me roaring away on the Harley, my other way to blow out the pipes, so the stationary deck becomes my armed fortress—against what, I'm not certain. Whatever it is hovers just out of sight.

Megan is born one delightful spring day in 1978. What a thing! Slim is excited but soon, and unexpectedly, overburdened with child care. Neither of us has been around babies much, certainly not enough to know how much our precious little bundle would change our lives. Although Slim has not been working, she has a busy life that she wants to resume.

This calls for action. We hire Desai, a young woman from El Salvador, an experienced mom whose son is waiting to join her in the U.S. after she earns enough under the table—no green card. Desai is very good with Megan and has a playful sense of humor that soon endears her to us. She doesn't speak much English, so our Spanish quickly evolves, including colorful cusswords. The aroma of her spicy cooking frequently wafts across the yard from the guest house, as does Latino music and TV soap operas in rapid-fire Spanish.

I resolve to help her get a green card. I hire an immigration law-yer who takes a hefty retainer, but the process takes years. Desai's son, Carlos, comes to the U.S. after Desai gets her green card and enough money to pay a *coyote* to transport him. Ken Countryman, one of the surgeons on staff, sponsors Carlos, who will eventually become a respected surgeon himself. Meanwhile, Desai becomes an ad hoc member of the family, the four of us living busy lives in Sierra Madre, California.

Now that I am a doting dad, Slim doesn't like me riding the Harley at all; it's one of our few true arguments. The day that it comes to a head, I have just ridden up from a noisy, heart-thumping ride in black leather and scuffed black boots. I park the bike and am fooling around in the garage when Megan toddles over and touches the shiny chrome exhaust pipe. Her screams bring Slim and Desai running.

I sell the bike.

One night, there is a strange—what? A malignancy?—that rides with me as I race my Porsche to the hospital at 2 a.m. to do an emergency tracheotomy. Sometimes they call me even when I'm not on call—I'm that good at it. It takes me three minutes, tops, to get the patient breathing again.

This black thing in the back seat is a presence that tickles my neck with pinpricks of poisonous intent. What is this? I see nothing but can smell something...or is it my overactive imagination in the dead of night? I push the pedal down and try to outrun it.

John, an oral surgeon, and Nina, his lovely girlfriend and eventual wife, are our best buds. We often go to dinner at fancy restaurants, the Chronicle in Pasadena being our favorite. The maître d' reserves a special table for us; the waiters, dressed in evening wear, bring our customary drinks without asking. John generally drives us in his vintage Bentley, or, on occasion, his Silver Cloud, for our evenings on the town—lots of them.

Sunday afternoons we four roller skate in the park with a picnic afterward, and perhaps a little Frisbee. We talk about world events, politics, love, art, and our own lives lived as our frivolity gradually gives way to, *is this all there is? What is it all about? Here John, take another hit, then pass it back.*

♦

That winter, Slim and I fly to Vancouver to stay with Anne and John, our Tahiti friends, for a week of skiing. We leave Megan with Desai, who has some prearranged backup and plenty of phone numbers.

Our friends' home is substantial and well appointed, with a basement guest suite served by a spiral staircase of shiny black metal.

That first night, as we sleep under goose down, I see the thing creeping down the staircase without making a sound. I am terrified. I sit up so abruptly that Slim awakens. "What is it, Dick?"

I look again at the black staircase, but nothing is there.

"Bad dream, honey. Sorry." Do bad dreams smell bad? I'll have to ask someone.

If the night had been black, the next day is blindingly white, the snow fields at Whistler sparkling with ice reflection and promise. We are all accomplished skiers and take the chairlift to the top. In a rare and embarrassing *oops*, I fall getting off the chair and have to reset my left ski. The others go swooshing down, leaving me alone at the summit, alone with a fear so paralyzing that I consider riding the chairlift back down.

Fear has nostrils and eyes, a mouth as well, but hears not. No reason appeals to fear, no words can convince. Fear is a mobile thing that floats along wherever one goes, hovering in the pastures of mind, eating away at reason, whispering with pursed lips, stealing wholesome breath then exhaling hellish fumes. Fear sees itself everywhere that eyes do roam, and curdles the blood with the devil's laughter.

Good Lord, why am I so afraid? Just then I hear a terrifying scream and whip around to see the source. I collapse on the snow with spasms of laughter. It is only a protesting pulley on the chair lift.

Well crap, I think, and ski down the slope with exuberant abandon.

Chapter Seven

The Screaming Yellows

No greater hell than to be slave to fear.
—Ben Johnson

August, 1979

At the Bradbury Building I thank Frank Kline for inviting me to his home for a recent Sunday brunch. It was a festive crowd; a backyard barbecue with plenty of beer and laughter. As I'm telling him this, I decide not to speak of the great anxiety that accompanied my drive across town to be there. I pause as I notice his blank stare. A few moments of silence grow between us.

"There was no Sunday brunch at my house," he finally says. "It must have been a dream." Then I wake up. The whole sequence was a dream...I guess. It's a Thursday morning, my Bradbury day. I call and cancel, still unsure of what was real and unreal. Increasingly, I hide things from Dr. Kline much as a teenager hides unruly thoughts and escapades from his dad.

Golf is the gentleman's game, and almost a requirement for ongoing success in many professions. The links hold power and keep secrets. Many a business deal, shady or otherwise, has been struck on a fairway walk or during whispered conversation on a putting green. *Ah yes, I remember we talked about a merger when we were looking for your lost ball in the rough. Let's go forward with it, my friend.*

So I learn to play. Gabe Gomez, a friend of Slim's and a scratch golfer, gives me pointers on the game on lazy Sunday mornings when others are stuck in church. Gabe tends toward good-natured cynicism, coupled with a Latino's resignation that I find engaging and colorful. He drives a beat-up VW convertible that advertises his persona pretty well. To say that we are good friends overstates the case, a fact that is quite helpful as future events unfold. It turns out that he would win more from me than a few golf wagers...but I get ahead of myself.

Frequently, I finish my day-surgery work by noon, usually tonsillectomies, ear tubes, or minor sinus surgeries, and I am done for the day. What freedom! I love sitting out on the deck with a few cold beers, watching the leaves of the two ash trees blow in the wind.

We have Heineken on tap in the house and a full stock of every sort of liquor that one is likely to see while sitting on a stool at a favorite bar. The only thing missing is the long mirror behind the bottles and a bartender polishing glasses with a white towel. I love drinking. It makes me feel normal and powerful, but the problem is that when I'm not drinking, I feel abnormal and weak—and sad. What would you do? Yes, that's what I did. I sat on the deck and watched the wind blow the leaves, refreshments close by.

One such day, Slim comes home from somewhere and, after giving Desai some groceries for her kitchen, steps out onto the deck. "We've got reservations at the Chronicle for tonight at 8:30, with John and Nina," she announces while plopping into a chair next to me. I turn to look at Slim, and her lovely face starts to wrinkle before my very eyes. I see her yellow skull expose itself here and there, crusts of foul tears gathering where her eyes once were. "What is it?" she asks with some alarm.

"Oh nothing, hon," I say, turning away. "I'm not feeling well, I guess. Why don't you go? I'll get something to eat here."

Slim is clearly upset, but just nods and goes inside to dress. It's not the first time that our foursome devolved to three.

The next day is sunny and already hot by 10 a.m. Slim leaves a note saying she's gone shopping with Megan and Desai. Such freedom! I'm alone, bathing suit on, chilled vodka with clinking ice cubes to banish my nausea from last night's party with Jack. An errant, unwelcome thought steals across the landscape of my suddenly disturbed mind: this is classic alcoholic behavior, this chasing the dog that bit you.... Fortunately, the rush of blessed vodka counters the unsettling thought with another: *This is your medicine curing your ills, better than doctors, better than pills.*

Hours later, my drowsy state is sadly interrupted by another disturbance.

For the past half hour, I have been staring at a small web of red capillaries on my swollen belly. *Oh Christ*, I think, *a spider hemangioma.* I jump up and look down at my belly again. Still there. I put on a T-shirt—gone. It's really not, and I know it, but it must be hidden along with the bell that tolls for me. I've seen plenty of these little red dots on the VA cirrhosis ward, the badge of imminent death with no resurrection possible.

The fear settles into my belly and mind, much like a dog dances around in a circle to make a comfortable spot, then lies down with a sigh.

♦

I pick up the phone with a trembling hand and call in sick— sick to death.

"Oh, just a stomach bug," I later tell Slim. Why can't I level with her? Why can't I be honest with myself? I'm just 33 and staring death in the face, every day a new torture added to my nauseating program, every day a new defense, a new dog-and-pony show required.

I look at these people that I love, Slim, Megan, John, Nina, Jim...I can't love them anymore; I'm not entitled, not able, not willing, not, not, not.

It must be Tuesday. I'm certain that it is Tuesday. I'm on my deck in my safe chair, but the chilled vodka makes me gag when I try to drink it, a retch that sounds and feels awful. I put the tumbler on the armrest and walk down to one of the ash trees and touch the rough bark, feeling the wooden pain of existence. I look up and see the blue sky between the leaves and branches, a color that no longer has meaning or depth.

Back on the deck, I try again. Gentle sniffs and sips, just a bit on the tongue to begin with, then my reddened mouth mucosa accepts the two-carbon molecules with increasing vigor, finally a swallow and no retch. C-C-OH, the organic basis of intoxication that has been my medicine has been converted-subverted into a dehumanizing opposite that is deconstructing my liver, big chunks at a time. This is my secret, closely held, carefully protected from the sun and blue sky.

♦

Dr. Kline is a bit late in opening the door to his inner sanctum. The anteroom has become stale with worry and I'm shriveled up into a knot of seasick complexity. He's cheerful but somehow restrained. Instead of confessing my miserable secret of impending death, I tuck it back into my satchel of grief and silently await his pleasure.

"I have news," he says, and, after a few bars of Beethoven's Fifth, "I'm retiring."

"Oh," I say with true surprise, Beethoven fading to funereal tones in the mist. *Did he say retire?* "When?" I ask, the answer quite obvious.

"Now," he says, arms and fingertips making a steeple, eyes peering at me over half-glasses.

"Oh." I grasp for a question that might save the day and perhaps my life. "We can still meet now and then?"

"I'm afraid not," words not well chosen since I'm the one drowning in fear. "How are you doing?"

"Oh, I'm fine, thanks." We solemnly stand and shake hands.

After I leave his office, I grab a shovel and begin digging. I start a tunnel at Third Street and gradually make my way under the freeway; dig, scoop, and empty, dig, scoop, and empty, occasionally popping up for an orienting view. The Pasadena Freeway already has a tunnel, I note, but I dig my own far beneath it.

The 605 rumbles above as I dig, scoop, and empty below it. Finally, I come to Rosemead Avenue where I surface and discard my implement. I flash out my right thumb and walk backward, and a group of hippies pulls up in a VW bus, music blaring, clouds of Mary Jane floating in the air. "Need a lift?" a young fellow with an English accent asks. He's colorful in dress with a long beard to his waist, and hair tied back. As I climb aboard he passes me a joint. "You look a little rough, mate, all covered in dirt."

I can't work anymore, this part is clear. I call Dorothy at the office and announce my first vacation, for a whole month. I don't talk to Jim for fear of an uprising of some sort, an unbearable thought at the time.

Back on deck again, my morning ritual begins anew each day, but there is another player on the field, a squirmy thing that floats in the air, an apparition that is fluid and ghastly with a face that looks like a gargoyle. It floats between the ash trees when my guard is down, quickly disappearing when I will it out of the yard. There is, to my horror, more than one. I can probably manage one, but what about more? Can I do it?

My thoughts on the matter are confused and jumbled. I know that I don't have DTs; they only visit when one stops drinking.

(Much later, I would discover that these nightmarish visions have a quasi-reality in the astral world, of which, at the time, I knew nothing. On the doctor level, I was experiencing the onset of Wernicke's encephalopathy, a psychosis caused by a vitamin deficiency connected to severe alcoholism.)

I am scared to death as death announces itself in telegraphed spasms of insanity that have color and mood, texture and feel, and leave me pockmarked with torturous loathing—the screaming yellows, I call them, unbearable assaults on my humanness that follow my footsteps from deck to house and from house to deck. The screaming yellows also hit me when I am up at night, the house silent and dark with insanity seeping up from the wool carpet at my feet. I watch Cal Worthington pitch cars on TV, a ridiculous man in a cowboy hat. His words are mostly about Buicks, but sometimes he turns and speaks to me directly, secret words that I cannot reveal. One memorable night my friend Cal took off his cowboy hat and puked into it, right on TV. I'd never seen such a thing before.

The OJ and vodka in the mornings seem to help. I get better. My periscope is up and I can see land. I actually pull my bicycle out of the garage and ride the streets of Sierra Madre a time or two. I'm very careful not to wear anything yellow and not to look at my belly.

"Say, hon," I say to Slim one day. "How about going to the Club Med in Cancun?" I feel like I've been ignoring her and know that this idea would be appealing. I have two weeks of vacation left, and we know an agent who could get it set up quickly.

On the plane I realize what a grievous error I have made. I'm really sick. The idea of food is anathema, but worse, the smell of vodka is so antiseptic, so revolting that I can't bear to taste it. My friend has turned on me like an unpaid loan shark that wants to break my kneecaps.

The newly constructed Club Med is a blazing white monolith in the sun. I see hundreds of black scorpions crawling all over it and wonder at this strange oversight by the people who run the place. There don't appear to be any venomous creatures on the walkway, but I resolve to wear flip-flops at all times.

The other problem is my low back pain that has flared and hurts like hell. Before we left I called my neurosurgeon friend, David, who came over to the house and gave me an epidural injection with me curled up on the bed. Painful damn thing. I have some samples of a new pain reliever, Tylenol, and start eating them like candy. It's the final piece of stagecraft in this drama that has me dying center stage.

"Oh Christ, Oh God—Slim, I'm really sick." She looks at me with sudden alarm and starts repacking our suitcases. I see her urgent talk floating in the air as she stuffs words into the black phone.

I start retching as the plane lands at LAX. I'm begging God to hold me tight until we get home, white knuckles clutching an airsick bag. Each moment is a red-hot squeeze that makes me ooze and gag. We are silent, the time for words long gone. I see pearls of sweat running down Slim's face as she drives us home. At last, my prayer answered—Manzanita Avenue, white stucco, red tile roof, home.

Desai is excited, Megan in her arms. Suitcases down. It all comes forth, bright red blood issues from my mouth in a spasm of gushing life. My head snaps back as far as it will go. I sink to my knees and stare at the ceiling as another retching red spasm spews blood all over my face and hair, a volcanic eruption with screams from somewhere. Desai rushes out of the room with Megan in her arms. I sit back on my haunches and count to five, then more upheaval of gore, but not as much this time.

I hear the ER doc on the phone to the surgeon on call. His whispered words are urgent and filled with alarm. "Yeah, I've never seen anything like it. Every time he vomits blood, his head snaps back. It's a mess. We can't get an NG tube down because of it." There's a long pause. "What? Are you kidding?"

The ER doc is visibly shaken. He comes to my gurney. "We're going to transfer you to Arcadia. He won't take your case."

He won't take my case? That's impossible. He, a casual friend of mine; he can lose his hospital privileges for this. Why?

Because you aren't in the right place, I hear. *Oh, okay then.*

Waiting for the ambulance to arrive, I insert the nasogastric (NG) tube myself. My mind is amazingly clear. I am no longer afraid and worried. I can think again, but don't take the trouble to think too much. I am tired. I lie back on the gurney and listen to the wails of the ambulance as I am transported across town. I am 33, right on schedule, which brings on the first mental laugh in a long while.

Chapter Eight

What Is This?

This world, after all our science and sciences, is still a miracle;
Wonderful, inscrutable, magical and more,
to whosoever will think of it."
—Thomas Carlyle

The ICU is always blazing with light, and always noisy. Always. Everyone except the patient wears green scrubs and is in a hurry, usually with worry furrows and urgent words spoken *sotto voce*.

I never expected to be in such a place unable to leave, wrists tied to the bedrails, various tubes and wires hooked up here and there. I really don't mind though; the medicines going in the IV no doubt having something to do with this unexpected calmness. I don't hurt, my mind is clear, and there is no worry at all. Blood is infusing in one arm, a cold sensation, while tired black blood is still exiting from my NG tube, the one I had put in myself. This has been going on a while, probably a day or two, and Dr. Reid is in and out, also dressed in scrubs and a white lab coat. For some rea-son, when he is in my cubicle, I stare at his name embroidered in red letters on his coat—*John Reid, MD*—and not at his face. He looks a lot like Frank Kline, MD: half-glasses, but more hair. Same smile.

His half smile is now interrupted with gentle words that I must listen to carefully to understand.

"You have bleeding esophageal varices, my friend. Not much we can do about it." He looks down, flips through the chart some more, and then looks at me again. "Your liver is pretty well shot. We could try a portacaval shunt."

It is my turn to smile then. The Los Angeles surgeon that had perfected the operation was none other than Dr. Mike, with Rich and I assisting upon occasion. I know about the poor outcomes and the miserable death that frequently follows. I think that Dr. Reid is relieved when I shake my head—no, not that.

A stream of visitors comes and goes: Slim, John, Nina. They each gave blood on my behalf and are now seeing it drain out the plastic tube and into a white container beneath the bed. Their kindness brings tears to my eyes.

Nina's thoughts seem to float in the air above her: *I've never seen someone so yellow.* And a few moments later, *I hope he doesn't die; I love him.*

"Don't worry, Nina," I said to her aloud. Then I summoned a smile and said, "You love everybody."

Slim was distraught and barely coherent. I worried more about her than my impending death. Dr. Reid had asked my permission to stop giving me blood transfusions after eighteen units had briefly spent time in my body before exiting into the white pail under my bed. It seemed pointless and, truthfully, I was tired of the lights and noise. The beep-beep of the heart monitor seemed to be an affront to my senses and, perhaps, to God's as well. I didn't believe in God much...perhaps a little. But no God, no Mystical Voice, would permit the sort of suffering I had experienced in life, let alone the horrific stuff of human history. I didn't expect that if such a supreme being did exist, I would receive much notice or help since my current situation was clearly self-induced. I blew it.

In this I was quite wrong. Blessedly wrong.

All my goodbyes said, except to Megan, who isn't permitted in the ICU, I am awake at 3 a.m. The clock across the hallway is silent, the tick-tock supplied by my brain as I watch it. I hear Mom start singing a favorite ditty of hers: *My grandfather's clock was too tall for the shelf so it stood 90 years on the floor...*

They had called from Indiana: *Should they come out?* No, I said for some reason, no need. Her singing was very welcome though. *...so it stopped short, never to run again when the old man died.*

Which reminds me of my own agenda. From high up, I look down at myself somehow, all puffed up and soggy with ascites, fluid in the belly that shouldn't be there. Yellow? My God, I am yellow, but not at all sad. No tears, no sir. In fact, I feel light and blissful with thoughts that are like birds in flight, gliding here and there, in graceful swoops and turns. *I love this.* I'm flying at last. I hear the beep of the monitor far, far away, down on the beach at Moorea where I pause and watch the playful splashing of people in the sea. I swoop and glide my way to Shaw's Cove where I see a Frisbee suspended in air, a lazy thing ready to descend to earth in its destined arc. How warm and beautiful I am, this Ichen. This is me, full of grace and full of bliss; fullness is my wonderful state. And then words form in my mind.

You will heal and work for Isa. Oh yes, I know this after all, and always have known. I am bathed in bliss. I am *love* with wings.

Another tick of the clock comes. My destined arc has returned me to Earth, alas, where I will work for Isa. My mind has trouble with *Isa*, which is a thing much larger than mind can embrace, much larger than God, which is big enough, my friend, but Isa is infinitely larger, deeper, and is *Mother*, for want of a better word. *Ha*, I think. *Nice to be back; this is the who of me back again.*

"No, no, Dr. House, you must stay in bed!" Two nurses are restraining me, but I manage to pull out my NG tube, the nasty damn thing.

"Okay, okay, but I need some water."

Two days later, I'm sitting up in bed in a private room on the third floor. No more tubes, thank God. Dr. Bert Peters is waiting for my reply. "I feel great except for a pain in my butt," I say, whereupon I'm upended for an exam.

"You have a large rectal abscess. "We'll have to open it today before you can go home." Ah, that magic word, *home*. Of course all my body functions are returning to normal and the bleeding has stopped. Everyone but me is amazed. I'm grateful, but also impatient to get on with Isa's work.

The next day, John Reid is signing me out. "You'll need to get the packing changed at our office every few days until the wound is healed." Then he put down the chart and extended his right hand. "I don't know how it happened—no one survives what you did, but..." He paused and looked me in the eye. "One drink of booze could kill you," as he wagged his finger.

"Thanks, John, I really appreciate your help. No worries, I'm not going to drink anymore."

The pain in my butt is intense but perhaps welcome. I am offered a wheelchair when Slim arrives, but I prefer to remain upright as I waddle out of the hospital and head for the backseat of the Audi. There are no angels singing that I can hear, but the sky is very blue, the smell of jasmine is in the air, and birds are everywhere, their sweet song a welcome earthly melody.

The house on Manzanita Avenue is a welcome sight. I pick up Megan and whirl her around, her squeals of laughter more pleasing than an angelic chorus. Desai's smile with a gold-capped front tooth speaks volumes, too; she seldom flashes it. *Home again, home again, jiggity-jig.* I put Megan down and walk through the house to the deck. It seems small and tight. There are no visions, no smells, just a wooden deck that affords a nice view of a nice backyard. The bushes need trimming and the guest house could use a coat of paint.

Everything needs a coat of paint. My practice has suffered in my six-week absence, but it's alive and breathing. Jim is restrained and tentative. He visited my yellow self and expected me to leave the hospital cold and stiff, not upright and enthusiastic about life. Always a gentleman, he carried on as if I had been out with a bad case of flu. Our cohorts at the hospital were also gracious as I resumed my duties among them. If I had been a good surgeon before, I am an even better one now, and love every goddamn minute of work.

On weekends, I go to the golf course and hit balls, but there is a tugging in my brain that I don't like. In fact, one day I am able to look at this craving directly: I want a cold beer. *What? After all that? Really?*

❧

The room at the Episcopal Church is filled with cigarette smoke, the aroma of brewing coffee, and people, some of whom are munching on Oreo cookies. At precisely 8 p.m. the chairperson, a young woman, calls out, "Hi, my name's Kelly, and I'm an alcoholic."

"Hi, Kelly," rings out the ritual response as about 30 of us find seats around folding tables, Styrofoam cups and ashtrays at hand.

As Kelly reads passages from AA literature, I am reminded of an Episcopal service led by a priest. True, she doesn't look very churchy and the people around the table don't look like parishioners, but it clearly is a service, and here I am, an interloper, a visitor. I almost get up and leave. I have Isa and don't need another higher power. But, my curiosity is aroused, the Oreos are tasty, and when my turn comes I am out with it: "My name's Doc, and I'm an alcoholic," with fingers mentally crossed. Even with *all that*, I don't feel like an alcoholic, with the awful smell and image that comes with that label. I do speak at this first meeting and actually feel better for it.

Bill Ward comes up to me after the meeting with the gift of his phone number. "Call me anytime, Doc." He is slight and a little goofy-looking, but his eyes are full of...what? *Acceptance*, genuine acceptance. The lack of judgment in his persona is his greatest gift to all the people he has helped in AA; that, and the off-color jokes that are his trademark. During the meeting, he shares a story about riding in a convertible on the freeway next to a prison van while a young woman performed a sex act on his person. That, I would learn, was vintage Bill Ward.

❧

At home, the more attentive I am, the more withdrawn Slim becomes. This conundrum is confusing and unexpected; I am seriously present and can be counted upon for husband-like behavior, but it goes nowhere, and we sit facing each other across an abyss of marital unhappiness. Undaunted, having faced down far greater problems, we start seeing Joel, a marriage counselor in Brentwood. These trips across town recall the early days of our relationship when we shopped on Rodeo Drive or took in an afternoon matinee. None of that now, the silence in the car only partially relieved by the stereo sounds of the Beach Boys and Grateful Dead.

Joel takes me aside one day as we leave his office after a spectacularly unfruitful session.

"She couldn't be seeing anyone else, could she?" he asks.

"Nah, it's gotta be something else, Joel," I tell him. Well, Joel's surmise proved to be correct, as I was soon to discover.

Sure, I'm going to AA meetings most nights, but that really isn't the issue. It's also true that I don't like parties anymore...me, the only sober one in the crowd. I could find little to enjoy as odd man out. But the real reason Slim and I are at odds is revealed after I agree to move into an apartment—a trial separation, as the euphemism goes. I find a one-bedroom rental just a few blocks down the road in Sierra Madre, an aging stucco affair with carports in front, typical of the late '50s. Inside, the apartment's many transient residents had left small portions of their lives impregnated in the carpet and white sheetrock, just as I soon would.

That first evening at the apartment after installing a hastily purchased bed and kitchen table, I go to a meeting and coffee afterwards. Poor me, I think, alone in low-rent squalor in spite of my best efforts; it's not fair, God, I protest. Instead of driving to my dreary digs directly, I decide to wallow in self-pity and drive by our big house on Manzanita Avenue. To my utter shock, there in my driveway next to my dark and silent house sits an old VW convertible—Gabe's, my golf buddy Gabe's.

Oh, *slings and arrows of outrageous fortune*, I am a cuckold. My heart hurts like a piece of burning coal in my chest. I gasp in the panic of upset. My foot slips off the clutch and the engine kills. Now I am a silent thing in front of the silence that speaks volumes; the dark house on Manzanita Avenue forever lost to me.

I restart the engine of the Porsche after enough wherewithal returns. No, I will not disturb them, for someone else lives there too: little Megan. However, I need to think about all this; there has to be fault on my part, too. Outrageous fortune *perhaps*, but Shakespeare's characters often ended up dead following ill-conceived action. I need to think.

My mind blasted into bits and pieces, I carefully drive to my little apartment and flop onto the bare mattress. I can feel separate emotions swirling around in my head, each vying for attention: betrayal, jealousy, anger, sadness, and a big dose of grief. I'm staring at the cracks in the newly painted ceiling as the hours creep by, anger flaring, then jealousy, then grief; who should I shoot? Gabe, Slim, or myself—no gun, that's a problem. No sleep, that'll be a problem tomorrow. Will there be a tomorrow?

What happens then, at about 3 a.m., is unbelievable. These swirling emotions, these unworthy thoughts, all *stop* with a suddenness that leaves me astonished and bolts me upright on the bed. What happened? Where did they go?

Now, I feel warm and peaceful, calm and serene, no jealousy, no anger, no feelings of betrayal. Nothing—all gone in an instant. How can I claim this? It can't be me. It must be Isa, no other explanation fits. After my experience in the ICU, I know that Isa exists and I'm part of something larger and grander than is ordinary. This second experience is so unexpected, so clearly beyond human contrivance, that the shock is soon replaced with wonder and excitement. Instead of jealousy, I now feel love for Slim *and Gabe* and not only wish them well, I want to be of help if they are serious about staying together.

I can't possibly go back to sleep, so I gather myself together and go grocery shopping at a 24-hour market. The night air is bracing, the parking lot is empty, and my heart is bursting with newfound joy. I take my grin and throw it around inside Ralphs Supermarket in Pasadena.

As dawn approaches, I drive to the foothills and hike up Eaton Canyon to the trickling waterfall. I find a large boulder to sit on and watch the sun rise over the treetops of Sierra Madre.

Slim, Gabe, and Megan soon move into a small rental house a few blocks away from the Manzanita house. Slim and Gabe had fallen in love when I was sick in the hospital, my death certain and imminent. When I had the bad manners to survive, they tried to backpedal their newfound love, to no avail. I assure them both that I understand the workings of heart and bear them no ill will—good luck and best wishes.

They eventually married and are still together as God, no doubt, intended all along.

We decide to put the big house up for sale and to divide the proceeds thereafter. I later pledge my half to Slim and Gabe as well, which is enough for them to buy a nice house together, plus some. In the meanwhile, I give up the dreary apartment and move into the silent, empty house on Manzanita Avenue with a "For Sale" sign stuck in the expansive lawn out front.

Such turmoil, such change, and yet I could dimly see a plan in it all. The joy and excitement that I feel on a daily basis is so enlivening that I scarcely pay attention to events that should have brought sadness and grief.

Big Mike at Laidlaw Harley Davidson is pleased to show me his inventory once again.

"We just got our first factory custom Wide Glide in," he says as we walk between rows of gleaming motorcycles that call out to me much like barkers at carnival booths: *buy me, buy me.* Mike then grabs a handlebar of the newest arrival. "Thirteen hundred cc's, factory flames on the tank, saddle bags, heel-toe shift," he says. I am transfixed. The painted flames on the gas tank seem to flicker as my imagination sends me off into the roaring world of black leather and biker camaraderie.

"Oh yeah," is all I say as I mount this devilish machine that's powered by testosterone-enhanced magic and just a bit of gasoline.

I wait while the mechanic installs a new muffler that soon brings forth the Harley thunder that is certain to disturb the peace wherever I might go.

Dr. House's Harley.
Photo © Kelly Taaffe, used by permission.

❧

It's Saturday. I'm sitting on the couch in the den after getting off the phone with an AA friend. Idly staring at the floor, I notice a sudden shift in the world. The floor tiles become illumed with enchanting beauty beyond anything I've ever seen. Gloriously beautiful, these tiles. I'm awestruck with wonder at this unexpected thing. These precious moments soon pass and I'm left staring at floor tiles of usual comportment. What happened? What is this? It is an exciting thing, but what does it mean? How can floor tiles behave this way? I actually become a bit wary of the universe that day: What's next? I wonder. Surely there is more to this story. And, of course, there was.

That night, I can't sleep. Perhaps the full moon or the incident in the morning has something to do with it. I get up and wander about the empty rooms of the big house that once rang with Megan's laughter. Desai has gone on to another position with Ken Countryman, a surgeon friend of mine, so her house is empty, too. I recall the smells of her cooking as I used to sit on the deck with Jack and his friends, the deck now empty, its nightmarish visions pushed into the void where they belong.

Back in the den where the floor tiles are still behaving, I sit facing the dark TV when all of a sudden I see a dark circle form in the air above it, maybe a foot in diameter. There is a pinpoint of white light at the two o'clock position. As I stare at this inexplicable vision, these words form in my head: *You will quit your practice and move away.* Along with this message comes a sense of joyful exuberance—of having received a precious gift of release, a ticket to embark on a wonderful adventure of some sort. I jump up from the couch, the dark circle now gone, the message lingering like French perfume, its essence so entrancing that I can't sit still. I pace the room, hands clasped behind my back, excitement filling my cracks with shimmering light. *My captain has spoken again.*

Without giving it the thought that it deserves, I pick up the phone and call my folks, who are now in Boston, Dad the chief of dentistry at the Northampton VA. Mom answers, her voice a whisper as she struggles awake.

"You're quitting your practice?" At this alarming news, Dad picks up the extension.

"What's going on, what's happened?" he asks with sleepy concern.

"I'm moving away," I announce with enthusiasm.

"Where?" Mom asks.

"I'm not certain yet." A long pause follows.

"Are you drinking again?" Dad asks. I laugh and realize that his question is more than pertinent.

"Aw no, Dad, I've been sober for over a year now. It's nothing like that." The relief in their voices is palpable, but I realize that the conversation is not likely to get any better. "I'll let you know how things work out." After I hang up, I can't stop laughing.

A few days later, I am walking up the steps to our office on Las Tunas Avenue, as I have so many times before. For me, work is a pleasure, something that I look forward to each day, and not a burden at all. Jim and I are on the best of terms and the practice is flourishing. Our new partner, Glen, is doing well, and the allergy clinic has expanded into another office suite.

This morning, as the sun is throwing color onto the low-hanging clouds, I unlock the door and realize that the mental message that I had been given is indeed true: I will soon be leaving, but why? Where? When? Later that day, I am examining a new patient and look into his nose at the inferior turbinates, a bit swollen, I think, when those turbinates suddenly jump out of the ordinary and into the extra-dimensional beauty that I had experienced a few days before: *beautiful.* I gasp just a little but assure the patient that nothing is amiss. As I pull back, the experience is over, the brief sense of bliss gone. "Well, everything looks fine," I say to the patient. "Let's see you back next week." *What is this?*

The residential streets of Sierra Madre are tree-lined and quiet, not much traffic except during morning commute. Instead of driving, I start walking the few blocks to town for incidentals and an occasional meal at the café. One Saturday, I am strolling along the sidewalk when the world shifts once again, the crisp sound of breeze-tousled leaves, the sweet smell of newly mown grass bring an inner peace that is so solicitous, it feels like God's embrace. Everywhere I look I see beauty. Everything I feel is good. There are, to my astonishment, no worries at all. None. I can think about *sources* of worry—finances, legal issues, lost love—but they don't inspire the least bit of worry; worry doesn't exist in this exquisite world that has opened its arms to me. I stop walking and simply stand in quiet appreciation of the beautiful wonderland that I never dreamed could possibly be.

I begin walking again, slowly, my balance a bit off. Yes, I can move in this world, but it requires directed thought. My parts aren't wholly synchronized with it; that's the feeling I get, more like swimming in invisible water, perhaps. Also, there is a constant hum that seems to permeate this world with a crackling sound when leaves stir in the wind. Colors are intense and vibrant—or is it smell that makes it so? My senses are somehow unified into a singular enchanting wholeness.

By the time I reach the café, the world has reassumed its drab shawl of ordinary weave. And that's the way it feels, that the fabric of the *ordinary* cloaks the beauty of a magical land existing beneath it. So intense is this feeling that I reject the other possibility—that it is hallucination or fervent imagination. In fact, the beautiful land seems more real than so-called reality.

Am I the first to discover this hidden world? Not likely, but why have I not heard of its existence? This mildly pressing question was not to be answered for a while, the fullness of the eventual answer more intriguing even than the question itself.

Another question presents itself: Is it all perceptual, or are there different laws that govern this magical world? I am riding my Harley along Colorado Boulevard in Pasadena with this question in mind. While in the right-hand lane going at a goodly clip, a parked car door suddenly opens directly in my path. Traffic on my left precludes any evasive action—I yell and brace for impact: *whoosh*, my motorcycle and I breeze right through the car door as if it were a phantom. I don't know who is more startled, the driver who opened the door or the motorcyclist who just abrogated Newtonian physics. My question is thusly answered: the laws are in fact different.

Where am I? Well, one foot seems to be stuck in the real world, and the other in a real-er world with different physical laws. Who am I? Ulysses? Cortez? Who knows? Even more important, who is my captain and what does he want from me?

Chapter Nine

Where?

*We want a few mad people now. See where
the sane ones have landed us!*
—George Bernard Shaw

My visits to the beautiful world become more frequent; sometimes daily, sometimes lasting hours at a time. I find that I can induce them by staring at a candle flame or by watching the lane markers pass when driving. Before long I can enter this special dimension by contracting small muscles in the back of my throat, a surprising development that gives me the sense of being in control of *something rational*, and that it isn't aberrant brain synapses firing on their own; this magical land actually exists and I have found a way to enter it at will. Further, I can leave it immediately if some interruption makes it necessary; it isn't a spell cast by some trickster to hold me in thrall.

As enticing as visiting this super-reality is, I feel no particular compulsion to escape the mundane world in favor of it. In fact, my mundane world has become less mundane with a gradual flavoring of it with the heightened awareness of the underlying reality, a spicy awareness that there is more to this world of ours than the unopened eye can see.

Oh yes, there are pressing concerns of the usual sort, the pressures of work and the huge sinkhole of lost love—I still love Slim and always will. Megan is old enough to understand that her life has shifted dramatically. Our visits become outings for lunch at the Hamburger Hamlet and trips to Lacy Park. I pick her up at the Montessori school some afternoons and we take walks while sharing our day. These visits leave me saddened with the realization that they will eventually end, that my life is about to expand beyond the comfortable borders of known routine.

The day is hot with Los Angeles smog browning the air and stinging eyes and lungs. After morning rounds and patient discharges, I head for the beach. A little escape is in order after an intense week of work. The air clears as I drive through Laguna Canyon, the fresh sea breeze announcing itself as I pass by Hobie's Surfboard Shop.

I have walked down the concrete steps to Shaw's Cove so many times that I feel a proprietary affront when something is amiss. This day a trash can has spilled its contents on the sand near the stairway, which has me muttering under my breath as I stop to restore order to a seascape painted by a divine brush and a full palette of perfect colors.

The sun is past the zenith but the white sand has retained its heat, making me hurry to the scrim of cool sand refreshed by each

breaking wave. The ice plant on the cliffs behind me is in full purple bloom, a colorful contrast to the orange nasturtiums along the
stairway. Could the ocean be any bluer? I don't think so, the white
crests of breaking waves rebounding high in the air with each new
set. No surfers today, I notice. Very few of us here today.

I walk out with a receding wave and find a seat on a high rock
that receives a light mist but is above the tumult of breaking waves.
Arms around knees, my long hair blowing in the ocean breeze, I
sit and let my mind float like the noisy seagulls overhead, the great
fishers of the sea.

What gradually seeps into my awareness is a quiet thing, a feeling, really, that has no words connected to it. I begin to feel a welcome state of bliss that soon floods my being with a peaceful calm,
the wind a blessing, the sea my comfort—God is in his heaven.

*This intense feeling of peace grows into an awareness of the exact
cloak and mantle of my mission on earth, my work for Isa, my raison
d'etre. I am floating in this state of awareness where mind and rationality are suspended, on leave and absent. I feel who I am. I know what
must be done and am humbled before it.*

It is a precious awareness that gradually dissipates as my senses
are overwhelmed by the mental buzzing of my rational mind, but,
for a blessed time, I exist in perfect alignment with that which I
was born to be—right here in Shaw's Cove.

I count the waves crashing on shore around me, five, six, seven,
a pause, then eight.

And so it is that I discover that which I am and what is to be
done. I shake off the aura and wade through the rising high tide
back to shore. I sit on my beach towel with arms around knees,
long hair tickling my shoulders in the ocean breeze, and think.

My rational mind does not like what has come about. The
mental protest takes the form of a many-legged creature that creeps
into bliss and trashes it: *No! This is a self-concocted fantasy and not*

from God. This is schizoid delusion, a sign of chemical chaos in the brain. You, sir, are a recovering drunk, a cuckold, and nothing more.

With these sorts of thoughts floating about, I stand up on the beach and start laughing out loud, for the ultimate answer—*is it true or not*—will eventually become quite clear; shut up mind, let's get on with life, one day at a time. I walk back up the stairs to Wave Street, get in my little white Porsche, and drive like hell back to town.

The Monrovia AA meeting is over, people standing in clusters here and there, the general buzz of conversation gradually fading as people leave the voluminous hall. I approach a young man, Bill S., who was somewhat of a loner and quite intense when sharing about his spiritual life. *Maybe he knows.* My curiosity was mounting—I had virtually no background in spiritual matters, other than what the Presbyterian Church offered. I had not read the Bible, had little interest in Jesus, knew nothing about Buddha, and had not heard of Mohammed.

"Bill," I say, touching him lightly on the shoulder as he walks out. "I have some questions about spiritual stuff."

He turns around, his brown eyes focused a bit above my head. He has an unruly shock of brown hair and takes little interest in his general appearance. There is some ineffable quality about him, though, that makes me certain he's the person to ask.

"Okay," he says, taking out a pencil and paper from an over-stuffed shirt pocket. "Meet me tomorrow at 2 p.m." He then favors me with a generous and welcoming smile as he hastily jots down directions before turning to walk away.

Bill S., who is a factory worker with a wife and young son. They live in a modest upstairs apartment in Duarte, a scrubby suburb of greater Los Angeles. It is with some apprehension that I arrive on Sunday for my first visit with the only spiritual tutor that I would ever have. Outside his apartment, I sit in the parking lot for 20 minutes or so—I'm always early—and gradually build the courage to submit my treasure for another soul's inspection.

"So," Bill says as he puts on a pot of coffee with a dash of cinnamon in it. "What's up?" In a gush of excited release, I tell of my experiences in the magical land that I deemed a different dimension, a higher reality. I do not share my experience in Shaw's Cove, which I have carefully tucked away in a mental lockbox that would not be reopened for a long while.

Bill sits in silence until I run out of steam, his hands folded on the kitchen table. He then gets up and walks into his bedroom without saying a word. He returns with a little book and plops it on the table: *The Art of Meditation*, by Joel Goldsmith. He pours us both a cup of cinnamon-laced coffee.

"Read this," he says, sitting once again. "You need to start meditating. What you are experiencing is real, but few people get there without meditating for a long time first." He pauses and sits back in his chair, his hands folded over his ample stomach. "Let's meet again next week."

And so it begins, my spiritual education under the gentle tutelage of Bill S., a factory worker in Duarte, California. During that first visit, Bill gives me three names that would prove to be important as my journey gets underway: Joel Goldsmith, Melchizedek, and Meher Baba. The first, Joel Goldsmith, is not only the author of the little book that Bill gave me, but had also awakened to a higher reality that allowed him to perform miraculous healings through directed meditation.

A few days later when I pick up Joel's book and read the first page, I am astounded—I know every word of it. Every thought, every passage, right to the last page. It is as if I had written the book myself. I slam it down on my kitchen table and start pacing the room. How can this be? After I settle down a bit, I take Joel's advice and begin a lifelong practice of daily meditation, first in a chair with eyes closed and hands folded in my lap, and later, on the floor in full lotus.

♦

As a young man, Joel Goldsmith was working as a salesman in New York City when a passerby on the street came up to him while he was on lunch break. "Pray for me, sir," was all she asked of him. Startled, he thought, *well, why not?* The next day she came up to him and thanked him profusely: *She was healed.* Thus began his own journey of discovery that eventually had him devoting his life to meditative healing as well as teaching the art of meditation.

Joel's books and seminars served devoted practitioners as vehicles of transport into that very land I had discovered—the subtle dimension beyond ordinary perception. He had not only gained entry into it, but was further able to harness the subtle power that comes from it, as his many physical healings attest. Raised in the Christian faith, Joel attributed his healings to the attainment of *Christ consciousness* and called his program of instruction *The Infinite Way.* It amazed me to read of such things, that the healing of physical and emotional ills could be accomplished by sitting in a chair and visualizing the afflicted person as restored to health, a child of God, perfect in every way. This was so contrary to my own indoctrination into the scientific medical paradigm that it made me dizzy with skeptical wonder. Had I not experienced the miraculous in my own life, I would have discharged the entire notion as wishful thinking or delusion. But I knew with increasing certainty that what Joel espoused was not only true, but also wonderfully attainable, at least in my case.

As I read Joel's various books, I begin accepting the notion that what has been happening to me is not as strange and weird as I had first thought: There is another world. There is a beautiful land, and I am learning to walk in it consciously—to what purpose is not entirely clear, but I suspect that it has something to do with the understanding that came to me that day in Shaw's Cove. I still choose not to examine these things too closely, beyond recognizing that there is purpose to it all, and that I am being guided by Spirit, whatever that means.

Joel found that he could only maintain his healing consciousness by staying outside of ordinary pursuits and living the cloistered life of a recluse for the most part, his meditation seminars the only exception.

In later life, Joel did marry. His wife, Emma, and he lived on the island of Maui where he felt his meditative efforts were greatly facilitated. He passed away in 1964.

Melchizedek? The first time Bill S. mentions this obscure biblical character, I get a tingling feeling all over and can scarcely hear what Bill says afterward. *Who?*

"Say, Bill," I interrupt, as he went on to other things, "who is this Melchizedek?"

"Well, there's not much known about him. It says in the Bible that Abraham gave him tithe."

"Where in the Bible?"

"I think it's in Hebrews." I make a mental note and resolve to get a Bible and look it up. Meanwhile, our conversation turns to other things. Bill relates a fascinating story about his former AA sponsor, Don Succup, who was a physicist at Cal Tech before his dalliance with higher dimensions and alcohol led him to the rooms of AA and sober living. Bill shows me a photo of Don dressed in a black cape sporting a goatee and looking like a character out of a play, his smile a knowing grin, his eyes flashing out of the photo like black jewels.

Don had pursued knowledge as far as physics and quantum mechanics could carry him. He then made the giant leap wherein mind is stilled and true knowledge presents itself far beyond the boundaries of mental constructs—Don found God and the heavens that are His realm.

"So one day Don asked me to split a pitch with him," Bill continues. "I couldn't believe it. It was a speaker's meeting and everyone was excited about hearing Don's story. Why split it with me, a relative newcomer?" Bill pauses a moment and leans toward me across the kitchen table. "I'll tell you why he asked me to split it. Halfway through his talk, up at the podium, he suddenly dropped dead. That's why."

Bill sits back in his chair, the distant memory of that day shining in his eyes. In a moment, he goes on. "After the paramedics came and took him away, there were still people left in the room, so I got up and talked about Don and his great love of God—and my love for him."

The next day I go to a Christian bookstore and buy a King James Version of the Bible, and upon opening it *at random* I find this:

> *Melchizedek, to whom also Abraham gave a tenth part of all. Without father, without mother, without descent, having neither beginning of days, nor end of life, but made like unto the Son of God; abideth a priest continually.*
>
> (Hebrews 7: 2–3)

Well, I don't know what to make of these cryptic words but I appreciate the fact that they have some relevance to my life—particularly in view of the magical synchronicity that had me open the Bible to the exact page containing them.

The third name, Meher Baba, is also new to me. Bill S. tells me that he claimed to be the avatar of God, Christ consciousness returned to earth. Further, Bill says that Meher Baba's lasting message to mankind was, *Don't worry, be happy.*

Upon hearing this nonsensical claim and advice, I shunt Meher Baba to the outermost fringe of my interest. "Is he in India?" I ask Bill.

"Yeah, but he dropped his body in 1969."

Meditation is an affront to usual mental activity, and battle lines are quickly drawn. One's mind wants to think, wants to create new thoughts, new desires, and new distractions, while meditation seeks to silence the mind's constant squawking. But what generates meditative effort? *Mind,* a smaller part of mind that tolerates self-destruction or at least self-regulation. It is a battle that often finds the meditator frustrated as general mind continues to churn in spite of one's best efforts.

Joel's technique is based on concentration, and perhaps a portion of scripture; his phrase *I and my Father are one* is an example. The concentration can then lead to exclusion of lesser thoughts and subsequent quieting of the mind. It is when mind is quiet that God may be heard, and I am quite ready to listen.

I sit in meditative pose several times every day. What I soon discover is that the act of carving the time out of a busy day and sitting for 20 minutes in silence is the most important aspect of my meditative efforts. (*This daily practice soon awakens the teacher who resides in each and every soul, including you, dear reader.*) What happens next varies. In my case, I soon drop the mode of concentration on scripture and simply begin pushing away thoughts. The thoughts that pester us constantly can be shunted aside even as new thoughts clamor for attention. These too are pushed aside. After 20 minutes or so I notice a calmness that is lively with blissful inspiration coming from deep within: I am centered and at peace. Such a simple thing.

In an unusual departure, I'm sitting cross-legged on the floor and not in a chair, the empty house on Manzanita quiet, the echoes of Megan's laughter now fading into nostalgic remembrance. I'm alone, yes, but no longer lonely or sad. Spirit has elevated me beyond human misery, it seems, my daily meditation bringing solace and quiet joy.

As I drift into centered calmness, my reverie is suddenly disrupted by a vision behind closed eyelids. I see Jesus the Christ standing on a knoll, long hair and pure white robe gently blowing in a breeze. His eyes are looking directly at me. I sense his love and great compassion—palpable forces that bind God and man together even as suffering is borne. It is His love that I feel and His majesty that I perceive.

I jump up as this vision disappears. What is this? I wonder. Jesus appearing to me—why? What I'm left with is the certainty that Jesus is truly the son of God, the Christ come to Earth on behalf of mankind. This I now know beyond any doubt. This knowing is not mind thinking, but knowledge arising from the direct experience of His reality: I know.

The strange part is my lack of connection to Jesus and Christian thought in spite of this direct experience. I can perceive no relevance to my life on Earth or to any possible mission that I might have. It is not Jesus that is directing the play in which I have a part. This surprising realization dispels any notions that I have about being somehow involved in established religion. It gives me the sense that new frontiers are waiting to be discovered beyond what Jesus brought to earth. Hallelujah.

My trips to the subtle world of such beauty continue both during and outside of meditation, the greatest treasure herein the total lack of worry while in these states. But, just like a switch thrown, the worries of ordinary life are there to greet me afterward.

One early evening the thought of cooking a simple supper is more than I can bear. I had already lost 40 pounds and am as thin as I care to be, a bachelor's cooking partly to blame. So, I'm waiting to be served at the Sawmill, a favorite Pasadena restaurant, when *time begins to slow of its own accord. A clock for wait staff is visible from my table, the second hand of which is lazing down, ever slower, as my waitress begins serving in slow motion, my plate of food descending to the table like an autumn leaf drifting to Earth. Slow, slower, then all motion everywhere stops, as does all sound—only the hum of primal existence coming to my ears. Odd, I think, to be able to breathe and move my eyes around to take in this frozen tableau. As I sit in an out-of-time capsule of amazement, everything is hushed, all is stopped, time withdrawn from its reach down into the past and up into the future. The suspense is blissful and not at all scary.*

Then, like a distant train approaching, I can sense time returning to resume its prominent role in earthly affairs. The clock restarts its circular march, my salmon steak entrée touches down on the table, and the waitress smiles.

"Is there anything else you'd like, sir?"

"No, this is more than enough. Thanks."

The next morning at 5 a.m., my meditation well underway, another startling vision presents itself. Mostly my several sessions each day are bland affairs, calming but not remarkable. Not so this time, for no apparent reason.

I see the entire world on fire, a holocaust of destruction with flames engulfing all that there is, the world we have known for so long now cleansed with the fiery breath of omnipotent God. The flames crackle and reach high into the dark sky. There is nothing to be seen but red and orange flames amidst whirlwinds of smoke and ash.

When I pull out of this horrific scene, it seems that I still smell the burning flesh of humanity, the grey ash still floating in the air around me. I shake my head and gasp at the enormity of the event. Can it be true?

I had not expected that a vision of this sort, vivid and alarming, would visit me, but once it had, I felt the truth of it settle in after a time. Yes, it's true, such apocalyptic forecasts have been with us since biblical days and perhaps before, the key question being *when will it happen*, and in this regard I have no clue. To me, the real question is *why* this vision has been given to me; my optimistic nature is not likely to have produced it on its own. *Why, why, why*—and *when?*

I begin to understand that I am being lifted out of ordinary life as these unusual experiences pile up. I no longer attribute them to fevered imagination or fanciful thinking. These sequential events have a certain rationality to them even as they speak of realms beyond human awareness. I am being led like a puppy dog on a leash—by whom or what I can't imagine. *To what end* is the real question that keeps me awake at night.

No doubt Jim wonders about my distracted air, but I am trying my best to be doctor-like even as my head is swimming with mysterious quanta and a dash of exotic spice. Nonetheless, we carry on, my patients increasingly happy with better-than-expected results.

Saturday lunches with Megan at the Hamburger Hamlet help to keep me focused on the important things—fries and onion rings. We laugh together and share secrets during these visits even as they sometimes end in tears (mostly mine). She is a delightful

2-year-old whose good nature could light up a room. This would be the case throughout her life.

Slim and Gabe are doing fine together, planning marriage when our divorce papers come through. I pull Gabe aside one day as I drop off some of Slim's things that had been left at the house. I look him in the eye and wish him well as we shake hands. He in turn asks me what my plans are. I'm certain that I startle him with my reply. "I don't really know, but I'm going to be leaving here one day." I pause a moment. "It has something to do with the apocalypse."

"Really?" he exclaims with raised eyebrows.

Oddly enough, I think he believes me.

The 210 Freeway is not as congested as its older brothers in the city, and I glide along at 70 mph without much concentration required, one eye out for cops. I hate to be late for anything, much less a one-on-one with Bill Ward, my first AA buddy.

I reach over and turn off the radio because something weird is happening. An irresistible urge has taken over my person: *I need to drive to LAX, get on a plane, and leave immediately. With this urge comes action: I press down the accelerator of the little Porsche and am soon hitting 80, 90, maybe 100 mph—I dare not look going at this speed. The engine is screaming; my ears protest. No matter, I'm on my way to LAX to get on a plane and go…where? I have no idea. My right foot eases up a bit as I realize the sheer folly of what I am doing: no suitcase, not much cash, and no destination. But wait, I've got credit cards and can buy stuff on arrival. My foot presses down again, 80, 90, maybe 100 mph. The no destination part kicks in again and I slow down enough to take the next freeway exit—somewhere in Burbank far beyond the turnoff to Bill's place.*

I need to think. My heart is racing, the urge still in force, my eyes looking everywhere for some sort of clue. I spot a Hawaii license plate on the car in front of me that leaps to the forefront of my awareness, bells clanging, mental lights flashing: THE DESTINATION. Moreover, there is a Maui decal on the car's window: Maui. So certain am I that from this moment on I have no doubts about it: Maui is the place.

I pull into a service station and park near a concrete-block wall about waist high that serves as a good seat for thinking. I dangle my legs and look out at the vista of California's asphalted strip malls and traffic lights blinking everywhere.

Maui. In spite of my love for tropical beaches, I've never been to Hawaii and haven't given much thought to going there. Now the idea seems very appealing: an exotic location that's not too far away. The *where* part of the question answered, the huge issue of *when* is keeping my heart beating at twice its normal speed. Should I obey this internal prodding and go *right now*? As strong as this urge is, my rational mind has a lot to say. What about Megan? What about my practice? What about the house payment and all the monthly bills?

As I sit there wrestling with these issues, it hits me that I have a surgery scheduled the next morning at 8 a.m., an ear surgery to restore hearing for a charity patient, Armando. If I don't do it, then it won't get done. Further, I need to be there for the post-op care. I can't go now. I can't do it; it's not right. I slowly drive back to the 210 and eventually arrive at Bill's place 20 minutes late.

God, the mental turmoil. I can't sleep that night, or the next. Have I missed the boat? Have I failed by not dropping my nets to follow Spirit's call? My meditations yield no answer to this most pressing question.

"What's bugging you, buddy?" Jim asks one morning as we leave the hospital after a scheduled thyroid surgery that we performed to-gether. We walk on a few steps while I mount a reply. "Well, the house on Manzanita hasn't sold yet. I'm still paying the mortgage and giving Slim enough to cover her expenses, too. It's tight." Jim nodded, understanding this worry, but I doubt that he would grasp my real concerns.

At 8 a.m. I dial the number Bill S. had given me for Herb Fitch, who happens to live in Kauai. Herb had been a stockbroker in San Francisco before his close association with Joel Goldsmith had opened up his meditative powers of healing. Herb had carried on after Joel's untimely death in 1964 and had moved to Kauai after retiring.

After several rings, I hear, "Hello?"

"Herb, this is Richard House. You don't know me, but I have an important spiritual question."

"Do you know what time it is?" he in turn asks.

I feel a rush of blood to my face as I suddenly remember the three-hour time difference.

"Oh God, I'm sorry. I'll call you back later."

"No, no, I'm awake now. What is it?"

And so it was that our friendship began. Herb assures me that I haven't missed the boat. In fact, he says, I've passed the test of Spirit—that we never have to step on toes to follow God's call. I did the right thing. Further, if Spirit wanted me in Maui, it would most certainly happen.

I am relieved to hear these words from this great man. Herb and I talk for a long while before he finally adds, "When you get to Hawaii, let's meet for lunch on my island in Princeville." My heart melts with this invitation and I get all choked up.

"Sure, Herb."

Bill S. mentions that there is a bookstore in Santa Monica, the Bodhi Tree, that carries nothing but titles devoted to spiritual matters and that I could find Joel's books there.

The place smells of incense with shelves and shelves of books, glass cases with crystals and amulets, colorful posters, flute music playing, and longhaired people ready to assist. I had no idea that such places existed or that the world's literature included such an array of books devoted to *spiritual quests.* Yes, that's what's going on with me, I conclude. I pick up a book about Buddha's life. I thumb through a book written by Yogananda. Yes, this is what's happening to me.

In spite of the treasure trove of literature, there is a certain resistance that I feel about opening too many doors. I buy only a single book, one of Joel's, and a packet of sandalwood incense. I seem to be learning about these things through direct experience and not so much through the written word—definitely a more exciting way to discover hidden truths.

Chapter Ten

Flux

*Nothing ever is, but all things are becoming.... All
things are the offspring of flux and motion.*
—Socrates (Heraclitus)

Herb Fitch has assured me that Spirit will open doors, but that
it is up to me to do the footwork. Then there is the obvious problem of finances, a problem that seems to dog us even in the pursuit
of lofty ideals. As I sit alone on the couch in an empty house, the
process of change is clearly underway...but how to make it all work?

The house on Manzanita Avenue needs to sell. It is listed at
twice our purchase price thanks to a housing bubble in California.
I have pledged my half of the eventual proceeds to Slim as our

settlement, but the house, forlorn and empty, has not yet attracted any buyers. Judy, our real estate lady, is a friend of Slim's which helps to energize the process, but, to date, no offers. Because I would receive no proceeds from the sale, my flight to paradise would require some fancy footwork indeed.

Maui. The dream needs some down-to-earth thinking, this much is clear. I apply for, and, in two months' time, receive a license to practice medicine in Hawaii. I open the manila envelope and hold license number 4051 in my hands. *Well, here it is, my ticket.* But, the piece of stiff paper doesn't come with specific instructions for use. As I feel the texture of it with my fingers and mind, I try to visualize the door that it might open. ENT—an operating room in paradise with me stuck in it? No, no—enough of that, I hope. An ER doc? Maybe. What else is there?

I carefully put the license back in the envelope as a nascent idea comes forward. I get on the phone to Honolulu and inquire about substance abuse clinics in Hawaii. "Oh, so there are only two? What about Maui? None there? Thanks so much."

Jim DeGrazio and I are more than medical partners; we are buddies. After almost three years of working together, our practice has flourished and the bond between us has deepened—a reflection of good will and trust.

The idea of bailing out and leaving Jim in the lurch is not at all attractive, to the point that, unless I'm walking in my beautiful land, I worry about it, even losing sleep over the prospect. One afternoon we're sitting in Jim's office and both of us reach up to take off our head mirrors, the signal that the doctor side of things could give way to the personal.

"What's bugging you, Dick?" Jim could easily read me, particularly since I'm squirming in my chair and fiddling with a pencil.

I look at Jim's concerned face and think about the many conversations we've had, with head mirrors on as well as off. This one will be a little of each.

"Since Slim left me, everything is different, Jim." He nods and sits back in his chair.

"I'm moving to Hawaii," I say as a prickly silence then fills the room.

"When?" Jim finally asks.

"January 2nd."

Jim gets up and closes the office door even though everyone else is gone. When he returns to his chair he has a faint smile on his lips, and I begin to relax. His fiery temper has apparently been left out in the hallway.

"I hope that it works out for you, Dick."

We talk for a long while about the details. Jim's offer to buy me out is quite generous, with a lump sum and monthly payments over five years. Of course, it is not the finances that bring such relief, but the fact that Jim is okay with the whole thing. Our new partner, Glen, would be happy to take on my patients, leaving Jim with few real problems. I suspect that he had seen it all coming and has worked out the details beforehand—he is a smart guy.

I have three weeks in which to divest myself of all my accumulated American possessions; three weeks to renounce my former life. I give stuff away mostly, with Slim and Gabe getting first pick, then friends, then Goodwill Industries.

Now the empty house is really empty. Not much left. Clothes pared down to two suitcases, my new uniform faded blue jeans and blue chambray work shirts—quite a shift from three-piece suits. When not working I wear Tony Lama cowboy boots and a western-style hat, or a red bandana when riding the Harley.

The only possession that stared me in the face and said *please, please take me* was a Persian prayer rug, two feet by three feet, and 10 pounds rolled up. Doable, but still a mysterious exception to my ruthless agenda. That and my Porsche.

The 1963 356 Porsche has quite a history, having been purchased in Stuttgart by my cousin, John House, who would soon become president of my family's clinic. John owned it for 10 years before selling it to me, its condition requiring a general restoration. Now six years and many happy miles later, I am forced to decide: sell, or store it up on blocks against possible use in the future. I am having trouble turning loose of it, and, unlike my prayer rug, it can't be taken along.

1963 Porsche.
Photo © Kelly Taaffe, used by permission.

The Harley is another matter. I decide to ship it to Maui as my primary vehicle of transport, a flashy roaring thing that provides emotional transport as well.

There are other concerns. I start saying goodbye to patients, a hard thing, and to close friends, even harder. My AA circle of friends has grown considerably and includes some whom I enlist as possible workers in a future substance abuse clinic. The prospect is quite attractive to those few, and their support lends a certain validity to the whole enterprise, as well as comfort to me. *It could happen.* One of my greatest supporters is Kelly, who would happily move to Hawaii; just say the word.

Each day seems to bring new difficulties, but the saving grace is that solutions come along with them. I learn to remain in the present where solutions come forth and not in the future where mental projection casts all the what-ifs.

The only exception is the damn car. I just can't decide.

And, lo, I am standing in the line at Taco Bell after a busy morning at the office when I notice a middle-aged man approaching. To my utter shock, he comes right up to me and says in a clear voice, "Sell the car," whereupon he turns around and walks away, never to be seen again.

I order my bean burrito and sit staring at it, my inner works in such turmoil that eating seems out of the question.

Of course, I sell the Porsche—back to John House in a fitting synchronicity that pleases both of us. How does this stuff work? Who was that messenger at Taco Bell? These questions don't bear much analysis, but the overwhelming sense that I have is of *support*, that all is well; my *captain*, whoever that might be, is guiding me and has agents on the ground as well.

There is, however, a glaring exception to all this wonderful choreography. One day Jim asks me to meet him after office hours, and, by the tone of his voice, I can tell that something is amiss. As I climb the stairs to our office suites, I marvel at the fact that in just two weeks I'd be leaving. I have my ticket to Kauai to meet Herb Fitch for lunch, and an inter-island ticket to Maui afterward. My motorcycle has been shipped from the dock at San Pedro and is on its way. Now, what's this business with Jim?

He is seated behind his desk and doesn't stand up and smile as is his custom. I sit too as a few moments of ominous silence swirl around the office like a forecast of stormy weather.

Jim pushes a newspaper article across his desk for me to read. I haven't seen it before. As I read it, I begin to understand: It is the report of a talk I had given to the Kiwanis lunch group about substance abuse. In it, I was improperly named as a sober member of AA, my anonymity blown by the reporter. Instead of Dick H., I was Dick House, a medical doctor in San Gabriel.

I look up at Jim after I finish reading it. His Italian temper is primed and ready to fire.

"What the hell did you think you were doing?"

"I'm sorry, Jim. I didn't know she was going to give my name."

"Now everyone knows about you. We could be sued." Jim is so upset that he walks over to the window and stares out at the dusky sky, ribbons of color just beginning to show. He then turns to me and spits out the bad news. "Your practice isn't worth shit to me now. I'm withdrawing my offer to buy you out." He grabs his coat and storms out of the office, leaving me sitting there with shards of broken dreams scattered around my feet.

The choice is mine. I can stay and fight Jim over a broken contract or leave it all behind and cast my fate to the wind. I continue to see patients at the office for another week and Jim calms down enough for us to stiffly engage again. I love the guy, of course, and he no doubt has similar feelings that were trampled upon when I decided to move on. Jim agrees to send me monthly checks for de-layed insurance payments, accounts receivable, for work that I had already done, but that's all.

I'm certainly not going to let a little problem like lack of money stand in the way of my quest. So, I shake Jim's hand with a tear in my eye and walk down the stairs for the last time. It is a cold win-ter's day with a light misting rain as I drive the little white Porsche to John's house in San Marino, and let the keys drop into his wait-ing hand.

Saying goodbyes has never been my strong suit; I tend to be stiff and too quick to leave; lingering making the pain of separation worse. Megan doesn't really understand that our visits have come to an end, but I get all choked up because I do. Slim wishes me well and I promise to send my contact information after getting settled.

Bill Ward isn't upset at all because he knows that our bond is unbreakable. We meet in his apartment for a dinner of pot roast and vegetables that he prepared himself. He is driving a taxi at the time and regales me with farfetched stories about the late-night fares he picks up—hookers mostly, he says, who use the back seat for business transactions.

In Duarte, Bill S. and I have a joint meditation for an hour the day before I leave. His healing presence greatly calms my fears of the unknown as I leap into the future with a couple of suitcases, a prayer rug, and little else—all based on a Maui window decal.

There is an upstairs lounge in the 747 going to Honolulu. I am sipping ginger ale there when the pilot wanders in to say hello. He's a friendly man in his late 50s, and as we chat we get around to my reason for the trip.

"I'm looking at setting up a rehab clinic on Maui," I say, "with me as the medical director."

He smiles and replies, "Bill Wilson is a friend of mine." We both chuckle and shake hands. This coded phrase means that the pilot is a sober member of AA.

The five-hour flight goes by quickly, the copilot flying the plane until we arrive at Oahu. Later, I begin my descent in a much smaller Aloha Airlines plane to a small speck of island in the brilliant blue sea below. As Kauai grows larger, I can see the green-clad mountains and white sand beaches of the Garden Island, a beautiful sight that sends tropical greetings to me as we land. Aloha ladies garland us on the tarmac, the leis smelling of frangipani, the beautiful flowers of the plumeria trees that are scattered all over the island. No wonder Herb Fitch lives here, I think, as I rent a Wiki-Wiki car to do a little sightseeing before our luncheon tomorrow. I ask for a map at the rental desk and the woman there laughs and says, "There's only one road." She does give me a map, though: Lihue, the main town, then Kapaa to the north and Princeville beyond. Outside, the tropical air is so thick that it feels moistly substantial and nourishing, clean and pure. As I drive with the window down, the breeze is almost intoxicating with floral essence and a salty tang.

To the right is the pounding surf of Wailua beach, and to the left, the Coco Palms resort appears with towering palms and colorful bougainvillea climbing up the low walls of the buildings. I turn into the small parking lot of this famous resort that has found its way into several Hollywood movies, most notably *Blue Hawaii*, with Elvis Presley.

The concierge is behind a rattan counter in an open-air foyer with Hawaiian music softly playing. I see pools of still water amid palm trees in the courtyard, pavilions and tables here and there, tourists wandering about with umbrella-topped drinks in hand. There are long walkways bordered by rows of tiki torches that are set alight each evening by muscular Hawaiian runners in loincloths, an entertaining display of speed and agility somehow reminiscent of ancient Hawaiian ritual.

My room is small, but air conditioned—an accommodation to the tourist trade. Most places are not so favored, I would soon find.

I walk across the road to Wailua beach and sit watching the turbulent surf crashing on shore, so different from Shaw's Cove. It is the same Pacific Ocean, but a different note of song and a deeper shade of blue. I nod my head in affirmation. I love this place. How much more shall I love Maui?

That night, my meditation is deeper than ever before; the sweet melodies of higher dimensions are more easily accessed. This is the best of all reasons to be here, I think—the beauty of the place notwithstanding.

I arrive at Princeville a few minutes early and sit in the parking lot with the air conditioning on. It is a golf course community with a clubhouse as well-appointed as any I have seen. The place reeks of wealth and exclusivity—not at all what I expected of Herb, who appears on the front steps at precisely noon. A further surprise is his ordinary appearance, tending toward ungraceful, even as his eyes bespeak great inner beauty. Herb is wearing a colorful Hawaiian shirt, shorts, and, on his feet, flip-flops—or slippers, as the locals call them. My jeans and cowboy boots are soon awash in sweat—a costume change is in order when I can get to it.

His handshake is strong and gives me tingles up my arm that last until we are seated at our table. We are soon picking at seafood salads and swapping tales of Spirit at work in our lives.

"You were right, Herb," I tell him. "I was escorted here by careful design. I just followed along and tried to dance to the music instead of running amok." He laughs and winks at me, his knowing look not requiring words.

After the meal he says, "I'm holding a meditation seminar in Monterey on the mainland in June. Come if you can."

I pause, wondering how things will be so far in the future; six months seems like an eternity—one day at a time. "Love to," I say, with as much honesty as I can muster. As this homely little man walks back into the clubhouse, I watch his retreat: a spiritual master in disguise, living among the rich, his true wealth and beauty well hidden by design. Herb Fitch.

The short plane ride to Maui fulfills my window-decal prophecy, but, as I explore the island throughout the next two days, I am surprised indeed. It isn't right. Not the place. It isn't home—my new home is somewhere on Kauai, waiting for me to find it.

I am tempted to look up at the cloudless sky and salute, but I don't.

Chapter Eleven
Kauai Intensive

We cannot be filled unless we are first emptied, to make room for what is to come."

—Thomas Merton

April, 1981

And so it was that my captain's call to Maui was merely the port of entry to my true home—Pono Kai in Kapaa, Kauai. And an exciting home it has become. After several weeks of the bipolar express, I emerge unscathed and ready to pursue the next challenge that might be placed at my feet—the feet that now have an urge to wander.

After months of strict seclusion I start walking the island, eventually developing favored routes for morning and afternoon jaunts. Sometimes it's the McDonald's about three miles away where I sit listening to the piped-in music and sipping mediocre coffee, never eating their food except for the miso soup they offer on behalf of the many Japanese tourists who are McDonald's fans, each of them carrying a camera to record the experience.

It is a longer walk when I turn right on the footpath, cross over the footbridge, and head into residential neighborhoods on the way to the Coconut Plantation resort and shops. The welcome smell of frangipani and jasmine along the way is interrupted at one house down the road, which always smells of the rotten fish guts that are left in the yard for the seagulls to clean up at their leisure. Perhaps it is *haoles* that live there.

The vistas of tropical flora on the right and isolated stretches of beach on the left make the walk my favorite one. This day, I'm sitting at a table under a huge banyan tree in the courtyard of the Plantation shops. There are tourists wandering about, some middle-aged couples dressed in matching Hawaiian shirts and straw hats. Many have food in hand, and I smile as a young woman frantically licks a melting ice cream cone in the tropical heat.

It is a very hot day and I'm grateful for my shady perch and the visual company of my fellows as they pass by. How different I am from these people, I think. It is with some sadness that I realize that I will be forever distant from them, never a tourist on vacation, always responsive to some higher calling. But, what exactly is it? What is this work that I'm about? I mentally shrug and begin the long walk home.

Although the craving for alcohol is long gone, a new addictive problem comes to visit: food cravings. Many of us develop a craving for chocolate or ice cream, but I start craving *everything*. All foods once eaten set up a craving for more; be it a banana or blueberry muffin, I want more and more until I'm so stuffed that my mouth refuses to admit another bite.

Good God, what next? I counter the problem by putting off all eating until late afternoon, "hungry" being the preferable state. Later, I stop eating anything at all except for steamed rice. This unitary diet seems to work the best and prevents the distractions that cravings for food create.

A dream: most of my nighttime dreams are of the usual variety, but occasionally an extraordinary one comes along. This memorable dream is cast in a golden light. *I see people seated around an ancient wooden table that is at least four inches thick and many feet long, of reddish wood with an oil-rubbed sheen. Perhaps a dozen people of all ages sit around it, some elders with long white beards, some matrons with silver tresses and purple robes, and even a few children dressed in woolen tunics that sparkle with pinpoints of dancing light. The mood is festive with lighthearted chatter and laughter.*

As I view this convivial group, I realize that I have a place at this wondrous table. One day I will take my vested seat and join them. When I awake, I half expect my beard to be white.

My Harley finally arrives at the dock at Lihue—a bit farther than I care to walk. I also have developed a bloodshot right eye with no apparent cause. I secure an appointment with an ophthalmologist and, for the first time, hitchhike into Lihue. Upon arrival, I hop out of the pickup truck with a "thanks" to the driver as a message from beyond forms in my mind: *never hitchhike again.* This time I give a mental *thanks* to my unseen captain and resolve to obey this order.

The eye doctor concludes that my red eye is due to wind exposure. No treatment required. This is the first of many such ailments that would visit mysteriously and then vanish. I learn to avoid doctors and their silly pronouncements, putting my trust in providence instead.

The motorcycle makes it possible to travel to more distant locations and I actually attend a few AA meetings scattered around the island. They tend to be lively mixes of wealthy tourists and local people, the disease of alcoholism having no class boundaries; a fellowship of humans on a spiritual course. I remain aloof from these people and consider my visits with them a special treat as opposed to the necessity they once had been. Had my alcoholism been cured along with the restoration of my physical body to health? I suspect so, but I'm not ready to test this theory, many alcoholics having perished after entertaining such thoughts and taken action on them.

Although I pledged to avoid doctors, I need to see a dentist. A sore tooth has made it difficult to meditate. Kapaa, as small as it is, actually supports a dental office above the hardware store. The waiting room features a colorful statue of laughing Buddha that lightens my mood a great deal.

After the exam reveals that a cavity needs filling, the Japanese lady dentist asks, "How much fruit do you eat?"

"Well, none. I just eat rice."

"I thought so. Your gums are bleeding. You have scurvy." I don't tell the dentist that I'm a doctor and should know better. *Scurvy? Good Lord, what an idiot I am!* As I walk out of the office, I can hear Buddha laughing at me.

I start eating fruit and veggies and feel much better. The food cravings are gone.

Another vivid dream: *I am standing on a marble staircase leading up to tall double doors. The doors are open but, in the dim light, I*

cannot see the interior well. I notice that I am dressed in a tuxedo. The clear feeling comes that I am to begin my spiritual marriage in the room at the top of the stairs. Upon awakening, the dream seems so real that I feel it is real, a peek into the future, as it were; not a dream prophecy as much as a translocation in time.

Aha, I think. There is an expectant feeling that great events are on the way, but along with excited anticipation comes a tinge of foreboding. Am I ready for this? The question tosses around in my mind during my walks in the morning darkness, the stars flickering in silent staccato above as I look to the heavens for an answer. It doesn't take long for events to unfold.

The house in Sierra Madre finally sells. Slim's voice on the phone is a welcome and nostalgic return to a life so far removed that it seems impossibly distant. "Great," I say with true enthusiasm.

"I'll send some papers for you to sign," she says, her voice a little sad—or is it my imagination? Perhaps the sadness is mine to claim.

The fluff of the new carpet has been compressed by my two feet in front of the meditation chair, evidence of my daily routine. It is therefore quite a shock, as I assume this familiar position, feet occupying the carpet footprints, when something unexpected comes about. I am sliding into that familiar place when, without conscious volition, my head snaps back on my neck as far as it can go. I am so surprised that I open my eyes for a glimpse of ceiling before I close them once again.

So, what is this? I had experienced a few spontaneous motions during meditation, but nothing this strong—or painful. The muscles in my neck soon cramp and, with my mouth open, I can't swallow. When enough spit collects and the pain has become significant, I think, *maybe this is an unnecessary aberration*, and easily bring my head down, open my eyes, close my mouth, and swallow.

I get up from the chair and irritably massage my neck muscles as I walk about the small living room. It is just getting light outside and I stand for a moment watching the sprinklers attending to their morning duty.

I sit again, whereupon, to my great consternation, my head snaps back once again, mouth open, eyes closed. Almost instantly the pain resumes; almost instantly my mind rebels. *This can't be right.* Pain was not included in my spiritual prospectus. My next thoughts counter this notion by recalling my recent experience with depression. That too had no apparent cause and was something that I bore to good effect—I got through it and was better for it. Maybe this is the same deal: something to bear, something to get through. I resolve to sit until there is spontaneous release, no matter what.

And it goes on and on. Hours pass and drool soaks my beard and blue shirt. The pain is so intense that small yelps escape my throat. My head is swimming with contrary thoughts. I start begging God for release. Surely it is God who has ordained this. *Please, please.* Then I start bargaining with God, or my captain, or whoever is behind this. *How about a goddamn break for lunch?*

There is no break for lunch. The red-tinged pain screams silently in my mind and I no longer can think at all. My knees are drawn up, my elbows flexed in a semblance of a sitting fetus, mouth open, eyes closed, wet, screaming inside, as the ambient light fades along with the sounds of playful tourists outside.

After ten hours in the chair, after all hope of spontaneous release has fled, my head relaxes down, my mouth closes, and my eyes open to the dim light of dusk.

I get up from the chair and start crying, tears flowing—for what I don't know. Buck up. I change shirts and go outside. The cool air revives me enough that I walk to the Japanese pines and find a seat on a large horizontal branch that overlooks the setting sun and calm sea. My right hand feels something irregular on the bark. To my astonishment, there is a carving in the wood of a human face with eyes closed and mouth open.

I stare at this image in disbelief. I run my fingers along the grooves in the wood—yes, it is real. Tears of relief soon spill as my heart beats to the rhythm of acceptance and gratitude: Nothing is amiss.

I sleep the night through and awaken late, daylight coursing through the screen door, my neck sore. Even before brushing my teeth I walk barefoot across the wet grass, across the asphalt path, and search out the branch that I sat on last night. Yes, it is still there. On closer examination, I can see that the image had been carved into the wood long ago, but by whom, and why? The utter synchronicity of the event took it beyond the rational and so far into the mystical that all my notions of cause and effect are blown into a tornado of whirling questions. These questions will have to wait, it seems. With hands on hips, I slowly walk back to the condo and the waiting chair.

It is only when I sit once again, my head snapping back with instant return of pain, that I realize this posture was the same one that had me spewing forth lifeblood some two years before. I could recognize a mystical connection between then and now, but nothing more; it was another mystery that seemed just beyond my grasp. The renewed pain flushes all contemplation from my mind as I settle into the tortuous day ahead of me.

The hours that pass are even more painful than the day before, but I have a towel to catch the drool and the clear understanding that there is purpose to it all. Moreover, it seems that my mind grows calmer as the pain becomes more intense. I learn to stay with the pain in the present and not to dwell on the future, like, *when will this ordeal finally end?* My mind also wants to explore the incongruity of my situation: I sit behind closed curtains enduring god-awful pain on a voluntary basis while tourists are outside in the sun splashing in the ocean waves.

I flash back to fraternity initiation, sitting in a darkened closet awaiting the series of tests—all voluntary—in the hopes of achieving mystical elevation to brotherhood and the satisfaction of having endured. I made it then and can make it now, but the current test of endurance has been amplified tenfold with no particular end in sight. I can't help but wonder how long it will go on. Day two also ends at 7 p.m., which gives me a comforting sense of order in a process that admitted little rationality otherwise. I gratefully stand, rub my sore neck, and fix a plate of egg-on.

On the morning of day three I walk to the footbridge and, while leaning on the rusted handrail, watch the sun rise over the curve of Earth, a huge orb of orange and bright yellow that soon gifts sea and sky with vibrant color. I slowly walk back to the condo with the hope that I can endure another day. My rebellious mind has a great deal to say about the prospects of sitting in the chair once again. The internal battle of will is quickly decided after I once again visit the pine branch for affirmation.

I sit.

As expected, the familiar posture reclaims my person, the physical pain no less intense, but as the hours creep by there is a noticeable difference. I feel less connected to the suffering, my mind now focusing on new input—pinpoints of light that flash behind my closed eyelids, a fascinating array of white points that I follow with my mind—ever more attentive to them and not the pain.

There is a gradual building of focus: something is going to happen. The pinpoints stop; I can hear my breathing beginning to slow. The pain has receded into the distance and I'm ready to accept what is shortly to come: a message, I perceive, from my captain, the Maestro who has choreographed this dance and music—the conductor who raises his baton and then commands these words into my mind:

I HAVE SPAKE.

Instantly, my head drops down in sweet release and a pleasing sense of completion comes. I'm done. So grateful I am that I give little thought to the strange message itself. *I have spake?*

The author in Kauai, 1981.

Photo © Kelly Taaffe, used by permission.

A monk in paradise.

Photo © Kelly Taaffe, used by permission.

Chapter Twelve
Marching Orders

The longest journey is the journey inward.
—Dag Hammarskjöld

The next morning I throw back the curtains and walk out into the sunshine, the sounds of awakening Kauai a welcome melody. A jogger breezes by as I turn right and walk to the footbridge, where there is an unusual commotion. A fishing boat has just arrived at the floating dock after a night-long trip from distant waters. The two-man crew is busy winching up their catch, a 500-pound marlin. The gigantic fish is silvery and glistening as they hose it down before the inevitable photo that would appear in the evening newspaper. The banter and backslapping fun at the dock is a musical

overture to the next phase of my life on the island: a phase of glistening reward.

Something has changed. I can see things more clearly, as if a
layer of dust has been wiped off of my thinking mind. I begin walking the island in earnest instead of sitting in meditation for most
of the day. After the strange message from God (or so I presume),
I once again sit in the chair, and, as I surmise, the painful posture
does not return—and will not for several months. I am propelled
into a new phase of discovery, the means of entry into it having
been vouchsafed to me by tolerating the voluntary torture.

The island byways become my meditative pathways, with insights coming to me as I walk. I no longer ride the Harley, which
I have secured in the bedroom of the condo after upending the
bed against a wall. My first walking insight is a startling one: *We
each become God.* The exact mechanism for such a thing remains
beyond my ken, but the certainty of this first insight is beyond any
questioning—it was and is a fact. It feels like I have read the last
page of a long book before working through the book itself; I have
the final answer but no details. The emotion connected with this
insight is amazed excitement. I want to shout this great news to the
entire world. What I do instead is write letters to Kelly and a few
other friends, no doubt revealing material that is less interesting to
them than to me.

I walk and walk, relaxing my monk's discipline to the extent
that I take in a movie on Saturday nights. The theater in the
Coconut Plantation is an hour's walk, the show starting at 7 p.m.
The first film that I see is a gritty, post-apocalyptic drama entitled *Escape from New York*, with Snake Plissken (Kurt Russell), the
hero, prevailing against all odds as he fights his way out of a hellish prison. A metaphor? On the walk home, I notice spontaneous
posturing of my hands and fingers—contortions, really, much like
those of a stroke victim. Because these movements are associated

with a pleasant feeling, reminiscent of my time in the magical, beautiful land, I am not at all worried—just bemused. It is on one such walk after a forgotten movie on a Saturday night that the second major insight comes, somehow connected with the strange posturing of my hands.

I must admit, dear reader, that I have no aptitude for math, and that the relationships between numbers have eluded me all my life. Nonetheless, the second insight is about numerology. I see with clarity that there is only one number, *number 1*, and that all others are contrivances that came about when time began. The next number to appear was 3. This marked the beginning of time when *1*, the present, was stretched into 3, past, present, and future. It was only when 3 was stable that 2 was possible, taking the form of past and future which, as a set, may be called *evolution*. The number 2, as evolution, became the creation in all its multiplicity but is entirely dependent on *1. Therefore, there are now only two numbers: 1 and 2, since 3 is 1 plus 2.* Our current computer jargon has put it at 1 and 0, which describes the same phenomenon.

Evolution in time comes from *1* (present) but manifests as *3*, past, present, and future. This trinity also supports another trinity: creation, preservation, and dissolution, which is the engine of evolution (2). As I realize the complex relationship of 1, 2, and 3, I feel my mind going around in circles, faster and faster.

This brings about the third insight, that the *thinking of God is circular, while human thinking is linear.* For the only time in my life, I can see the direct pathway to insanity: becoming lost in the circular play of numbers where linear thinking oscillating with circular thinking can destroy the human intellect. I mentally put up a sign: *Do not pass this point*, and, without difficulty, I have not.

The beauty of these insights isn't lost on me, but I know that there is a great deal more. I truly have read the last page in the book and wonder, as I wander, how the rest of the story will present itself—as I know without a doubt that it will.

Although I sleep on the couch in the living room where the sounds of the waves are audible, I rarely sit on it. A departure from the ordinary finds me relaxing there when a sudden urge brings me to me feet. Without any conscious volition, my feet carry me outside in a gliding walk that requires no effort at all. I am on some sort of autopilot, it seems, with some purpose to it. I'm very happy to follow along as the captain leads me...where?

My feet turn me right on the asphalt path, the afternoon sun shining brightly above. Over the footbridge I go, noticing that no boats or crew are around. There are a couple of young boys swimming in the river, but I do not wave to them as I usually would.

It actually feels like I'm gliding on a magic carpet, the sea breeze gently blowing me along. Down the path about 50 yards, my feet abruptly turn left and walk me through brush and sea grass down the slope toward the beach below. I'm amazed at my surefootedness as I quickly hike downward through rocks and driftwood, as if my feet have eyes of their own. Once on the beach, I walk directly to the wet sand, the incoming waves just touching my flip-flops and toes. My head then jerks upward a bit and my eyes focus on a distant object bobbing in the clear blue water. Can it be a bottle? I stand transfixed... Yes, it is a bottle, which soon is caught up in the breaking waves, each one bringing it closer to shore. The sea breeze brings the smell of seaweed and salt air to my nostrils as my toes gradually sink into the wet sand with each incoming wave. I patiently await the bottle's pleasure.

I can hardly believe what is happening as the re-corked wine bottle finally floats right up to my half-buried sandals and toes, an obvious message-in-a-bottle fairytale playing out. I fully expect to find a note addressed to me inside as I reach down to pick it up. Alas, there is no note; it's empty.

I stand a moment, bottle in hand, and let my half-stilled mind think. *Aha, there* is *a message*, but to receive it I must return to the

couch. Now, I toss the bottle back into the surf to resume its mind-
less journey, and I pull my feet out of the sand and allow them to
glide me back home and to the waiting message.

My gliding walk takes me back to the condo and couch where
it all began. I have enough sense to remain there and not switch to
the meditation chair, but I do close my eyes and quietly wait. What
comes then in the quiet stillness of my mind is one word: *Brisbane*.
My message in a bottle.

Brisbane? I jump up and pace the floor trying to recall...Brisbane.
A city in Australia? I think so. It being Sunday, the small island
library is closed, and by the time I arrive there the next morning, I
am relatively certain that Brisbane is a city in Australia, and, moreover, that I should go there. The reference librarian confirms my
thought: Brisbane is a city on the east coast in Queensland, north
of Sydney, Australia.

Back at the condo I am sitting at the kitchen table, my mind
swirling with thoughts about what has transpired. The phone rings;
it is Mr. Connor, the hospital director. "Dr. House?"

"Yes, hello."

"I'm sorry it took so long, but the board has reviewed your
proposal for starting a substance abuse program." He paused as I
heard him shuffle some papers. "Basically, we agree that the hospital should go forward with it."

"That's great."

"With you as medical director. It'll take a few months to get a
new wing built. I'll call you when the plans are ready."

A week later, I call Herb Fitch in Princeville to tell him I will
be leaving for Australia soon. We have enjoyed a few lunches together in the past months and he now suggests a parting one, to

which I readily agree. I shine up the Harley in preparation for sale and resolve to ride it one last time.

The roar of the motorcycle and the blast of hot wind in my face gives me a euphoric feeling of power and movement.

Leave this place? The choice isn't really a choice. True, I could easily spend the rest of my life in paradise, could be the good doctor helping people on the path to sobriety. Respect, authority, financial security, perhaps even love might await me at the end of the rainbow here on the Garden Isle. Nevertheless, as soon as I heard the word *Brisbane*, I started mentally packing my bags. I call Mr. Connor and wish him good luck, telling him that the project should go forward in my absence. I remind him that there is good AA on the island and name an Episcopal priest who has an interest in helping the project get started.

We meet at Herb's home on the golf course and once again I marvel at the incongruity. A wealthy retired stockbroker, Herb spends his days focused on spirit and meditative healing. I don't think he plays golf.

As we eat a simple meal, I give Herb a brief overview of my recent experiences without going into much detail—just enough for him to understand why I'm leaving.

"What's in Brisbane?" Herb sagaciously asks.

"I have no idea, Herb, but it's very clear that I should go there."

He looks at me intently. "Yes, yes, you should."

I ask about his upcoming seminar in Monterey. It is two weeks hence and I vow to be there if I can find a buyer for the Harley, money being tight. He smiles but doesn't offer a discount on the seminar fee.

I admit it: I am worried about selling the Harley. The mechanic at the motorcycle shop said it had to be the only Harley Davidson on the island, smaller Japanese bikes being more favored. *Good luck,* he had said. The ad in the paper has been running for a week without any response at all and I am losing sleep over it.

These cloudy thoughts are disturbing my serenity as I sit on the rock jetty watching a huge log bouncing around in the surf. Maybe 20 feet long, it seems resistant to coming in to shore, each set of waves bringing it closer, then farther away, a watery dance of log and sea.

Just then, a young man backs up a dull green Army surplus truck on the beach next to the dock. He hops out and stretches a steel cable out from the crane on the back in an effort to lasso the floating log. Entranced, I sit watching for the next hour until he finally manages to secure the log without getting crushed in the process. The whirring sound of the winch and straining truck engine is so different from the usual beach harmonies. The entire scene is remarkable as he's finally able to pull the log up onto the bed of the huge truck.

I walk over and find the young man humming a tune as he ties down the log.

"What are you going to do with it?" I ask.

"I'm a carver. It's free hardwood of some sort. I'll make good use of it."

I nod and wander back to my seat, realizing that I was probably more worried about the outcome of his struggle than he was. It is at this point that I realize how much worry interferes with happiness. In a flash, I recall Bill's mention of Meher Baba, whose great pronouncement was, "Don't worry, be happy." Aloud I say to the rocks on the jetty, "Well, maybe I should read about this guy."

The librarian says that none of the libraries in Hawaii have any books about Meher Baba; I would have to look on the mainland. Because I hope to be there very soon, I make a mental note to do so and sit by the phone waiting for a buyer to call. And I worry.

At the McDonald's one afternoon, I am sipping a cup of tepid coffee when a piped-in tune snares my attention: *It happened in*

Monterey, a long time ago... I jump up and half-jog back to the condo. The phone rings. A fellow asks a few questions about the Harley and offers to buy it at full price, sight unseen.

The travel agent in Lihue, a *haole* woman a few years older than I, is clearly taken with the task I present her.

"Is that a roundtrip ticket to Brisbane?"

"Ah, no, I don't think so," I say. "Let's make it a two-month stay, and then I'm going to India September 10th." I am startled to learn of this plan as I voice it. Why India?

"And after that?" she asks.

"Perhaps London." I drum my fingers on the desk. "Yes, London for a month."

"And then?"

"New York City." No longer concerned, I let it flow, this plan that has me circling the globe.

The price of airfare is almost exactly what I received from the sale of the Harley. In a sense my motorcycle was taking me around the world. I also secure a flight to the mainland to attend Herb's meditation seminar.

It happened in Monterey, that old Spanish town...

Another dream: *I'm standing in a cobblestoned plaza where there are several stores. Ivy grows up one brick-faced storefront. The sign above the door is almost obscured by the ivy, but I see that it says Natural Shoes. The dream is suffused with a golden light, and I'm very much drawn to this store and decide to go in just as the dream and the beautiful light fade.*

Upon awakening, I understand that the dream store is in Pasadena and I resolve to search it out. Its reality not in much question, the only imponderable is, why?

❧

LAX, one of the busiest airports in the world, is noisy, smelly, and casts a spell of urgency that is hard to shake off. I'm not really in a hurry, but get caught up in the moving tide of competitive people scrambling for position in one line or another.

Standing at curbside with a small daypack, I finally board a Dollar Rent-A-Car van that takes several of us to a remote lot and another line.

I used to live here, I think, as I patiently wait for the next unsmiling agent.

Eventually, a small Pontiac Sunbird and I make our way down the 405 to the Harbor, then to Pasadena Freeway. More like a concourse road-race than a freeway, the Pasadena requires nerve and alertness that I can barely muster, my reflexes dulled by island life and my consciousness so open that sensory input is multidimensional. I wonder about dealing with such things as navigation and actually engaging with people once again.

I put these concerns aside and concentrate on the tasks at hand. The Orange Grove exit leads me to Pasadena to begin my search for the dream store, should it exist.

Cruising down Colorado Boulevard, I remember a nice lunch spot, the Green Street Café, and I park a few blocks away. It is quite warm and I'm grateful for the shade of the large ficus trees as I stroll along the sidewalk. Perhaps I shouldn't be surprised, but as I approach the café I come upon the very cobblestone plaza that was in my dream. I stand looking at the scene before me, which includes the sign *Natural Shoes*. How does this work? Maybe I shouldn't even ask. What is clear to me is the fact that I should enter the store, which I do.

"May I help you?" a young woman asks.

"Yes, what are these sandals?"

"Birkenstocks. From Germany." I pick up a pair, concluding that they are unusually ugly and quite pricey.

"Okay, fix me up with a pair," I say, noting that the store carries no other shoes. Someone has gone to a lot of trouble to get me here. Birkenstocks must have some hidden utility to justify all this. I slide into my new sandals and walk over to the Green Street Café to get some lunch.

After searching local bookstores, a clerk finally directs me to the Meher Baba Bookstore in L.A. on Santa Monica Boulevard, about an hour's drive away. Once there, it appears somewhat shabby on the outside, giving me pause. *Should I go in?*

I sit a moment before venturing up the concrete steps. As I open the door, the smell of sandalwood incense tickles my nostrils. Inside, there are tables and shelves filled with books and pamphlets. I turn my gaze to the right where a picture of Meher Baba hangs. He is smiling right down at me—for good reason. He is laughing at me as I look into his eyes. He is, I immediately know, the very captain who has been orchestrating my journey. *He* is behind it all. I stand rooted as my mind and heart absorb this surprising development. There is no doubt whatsoever, just wonder, just incredible surprise.

I notice a portly man of middle age approaching.

"May I help you?" he asks, hands clasped together. "I am Dana Field." I tear my attention from the photo and turn to him. There are so many questions that I simply reach up and grab the nearest one. "Is he married?"

"Oh, no, Baba was chaste all his life. The great love of his life, Mehera, was also chaste."

"India, right?"

"Baba traveled all over the world, but, yes, his home was near Poona [Pune], India."

"Who is he?" I ask.

"The avatar, Christ consciousness on Earth. He *said* he came to Earth to awaken mankind, although he was actually silent. He used gestures to communicate. He didn't utter a word for 50 years, but promised that when he broke his silence the new age would dawn."

"Is he still alive?"

"He dropped his body in 1969, but he retains awareness of the creation for one hundred years after that." *Well, from my standpoint, he is not only aware of the damn creation, but is dragging me around in it.* I don't say these words aloud.

I nod as my mind continues its red-hot dance. I look around the store and half-yell at Dana, "I want one of every book and pamphlet that you have here." There must have been 20 or 30 in various sizes and shapes, all of them about this one soul—my captain, now unveiled.

As Dana starts packing books, I turn to look at the photo of Meher Baba once again: about 60 years old, with deep, dark eyes with heavy eyebrows, dark hair pulled back, a big mustache beneath a prominent nose, and a knowing smile. There is such compassion and gentleness about him that all my senses are calmed by his appearance. *This is the guy*, my heart proclaims once again. It's a shocking and wonderful thing; a certainty that would only grow with time and experience.

I turn to Dana and say, "I'll take a few books with me. Can you ship the rest?"

"Sure. Where?" I give him my Kauai address but admonish him to hurry, that I'm leaving in two weeks for Brisbane, Australia.

"Brisbane?" he says. "Do you know about Avatar's Abode near Brisbane?" I turn to face Baba's picture and imagine him laughing again, slapping his thigh in mirth.

"No," I reply. "Tell me."

It turns out that Meher Baba established three primary centers for his work on Earth: Ahmednagar, India; Woombye (near Brisbane), Australia; and Myrtle Beach, South Carolina. Upon learning this, I make a mental note to add Myrtle Beach to my itinerary. Dana gives me Bill Le Page's address at Avatar's Abode and suggests that I write to him about my upcoming visit.

Before I leave, Dana wants to hear my story, how it all came about. At this point, I am sufficiently addled that I don't remember what I said. I do recall that he took some notes, and I remember relating the *Do not worry...* part of the tale.

On the way out of town, the Hollywood Freeway takes me past the monolithic County Hospital. Was I really a doctor there once? Seems pretty farfetched now, the truer reality of the present quest so far removed from blood and guts that I shake my head in wonder. Who the hell am I, anyway?

I press the pedal down and the Sunbird and I rocket out of L.A. along the coast. Many hours later, after negotiating Big Sur, I arrive in Monterey, the fishing village immortalized in John Steinbeck's novel *Cannery Row*. Now a popular tourist destination and living habitat for noisy sea lions, there remains a wistful feel to the place, a calmness even, that makes it a good choice for group meditation.

Herb is up front incanting gentle phrases as about 60 of us sit in stillness. Group meditation can be quite powerful, and as I peek about, I see well-dressed matrons for the most part, and some men too. I must be the youngest here, and I can't be still in spite of the soporific phrases that Herb floats around the room. If he hadn't been a friend, I would have exited forthwith.

It is a three-day marathon with my true interest riveted in the books I read in the evenings. The ancient Vedic and Sufi teachings in them fill in the huge gaps in my understanding of how things really work. The Sufis are little known in the United States, although their presence here dates to the 1920s, when the great Sufi master Inayat Khan brought this ancient teaching to our shores. The Sufis are thought to be the holders of universal truths that have been carefully guarded and then taught to initiates from the earliest days of mankind. Currently, the Sufis are connected to the mystical branch of Islam, while in the past they were thought to be the Essenes of biblical note, perhaps responsible for teaching Jesus during his unaccounted years. The Sufis have an ongoing, direct connection to the avatar in each incarnation and preserve traditions and truths in between advents.

Vedic scriptures gave rise to Hinduism and go back to the ancient days of India; although seen from a different perspective, the basic teachings and truths are the same ones espoused by the Sufis. In our current Earthly cycle of time, perfect masters have been aligned with either one of these two ancient traditions.

Perfect masters? Presbyterian theology doesn't admit to any such thing. My initial resistance quickly gives way to intense curiosity as I read page after page, burning the midnight oil.

Yes, I conclude, it makes sense. There are always five souls on Earth who are one with God and whose consciousness has been perfected over countless lifetimes. I call them Guardians. Reincarnation? Yes, I had accepted that notion long before. It's the only way that the vagaries of human life make sense: some rich, some poor, some healthy, some not. We experience *all of it* at one time or another, forgetting past lives as we assume a new one.

Sufi and Vedic thought agree that when humankind needs a spiritual push, the five perfect masters—Qutub in the Muslim tradition or sadguru in the Hindu tradition—call down the first-ever soul to achieve union with God, the Ancient One, who is reborn on Earth as the Christ, the avatar of God, not once, but every 700 to 1,400 years to reorder the affairs of mankind.

Periodically, I put the reading aside—it is a lot to process at once. I walk the quiet streets of Monterey where night sounds echo through the misty air, the faint smell of fennel—wild licorice—giving the air a tangy substance.

The night clerk at the Double Tree Inn nods each time I pass by, probably wondering about my nocturnal walks. I consider stopping to chat with him and fantasize about telling him how things really work—perfect masters and all—but I don't. In fact, I intuitively know that this level of information should only be shared with people prepared to accept it, those on a spiritual quest themselves. Our sad history of burning mystics alive speaks to this issue and prods me to keep my mouth shut, even as I keep my mind open.

Oh, there is more, a great deal more, and, like a tonic, the newly acquired information fills my heart with excited glee and disallows any sleep whatsoever. I feel like a man who happens upon a half-buried pirate's chest on the beach and opens it to discover *pieces of gold* for the taking: I scurry off with handfuls of them under my shirt, holding them close to my heart. What treasure!

Herb Fitch is too involved with his seminar folks to do more than say a fond goodbye as we hug in the lobby. I assure him that I will keep in touch and, as he walks away, his brightly colored Hawaiian shirt receding into the distance, I know that it is to be our last meeting.

Back on Kauai, I resume my reading, and walk, and walk, this time in Birkenstocks, my chronically sore flat feet now happy for the first time ever.

Awareness grows.

It doesn't take long for me to put it together. The strange message I had received at the end of my ordeal in the chair, I HAVE SPAKE, was in reference to Meher Baba's silence begun in 1925. He was a young man of 31 then, and had a group of devoted followers—*mandali* he called them—who wondered at his sudden vow. "Why?" they asked him. His written answer declared that his mission was to awaken mankind from its deep slumber of ignorance—to allow all people to experience divine love on Earth, that the saints and sages had given the world plenty of words to ponder but that true knowledge is given and received in silence.

As the years went by Baba further declared that when he breaks his silence, soon afterward a great cataclysm will befall Earth and three-fourths of mankind will perish. This in turn will herald the dawning of the new age, the Age of Aquarius, when each soul on earth will be directly aware of divine presence and love.

Meher Baba exasperated his many followers by predicting that he would soon *break his silence*...only to postpone it. He maintained complete silence until his death 50 years later, first communicating by writing on a paper tablet, and then on an alphabet board that had him pointing to individual letters at lightning speed, smiling all the while, his mandali deciphering the words as they appeared. In this manner he dictated three entire books, *God Speaks*, *Discourses*, and *Beams from the Spiritual Panorama*.

Later, he gave up the alphabet board in favor of stylized finger and hand gestures that the mandali learned to read. Many people who first met Baba were so taken with his presence they didn't notice that it wasn't he who spoke, but someone behind him.

So, what does I HAVE SPAKE mean in context? I'm not certain. It is clear to me that I am caught up in momentous events and mysterious goings-on, but that's it.

About halfway to the Coconut Plantation on one of my afternoon walks, I am brought up short by an unusual sight. There on the beach a local family has set up a tent and, in spite of the summer heat, has a campfire going. Several children are splashing in the waves while others are cooking hotdogs over the driftwood fire.

Camping in Kauai? I hadn't seen it before, and the sight carries a thought that enters my mind like an urgent telegram from beyond: *I should buy camping gear and a backpack for a walk across India.*

So strong is this notion that I have trouble not thinking about it. Actually, my only concern—replacing all others—is what gear to get, and where. I continue my walk to Coconut Plantation, but, instead of watching the passersby, I enter the shops in a search of camping gear. To my surprise, I find a few items at an equestrian shop, including a large leather satchel and a water bottle. It is only after I have purchased these items that my logical mind kicks in. *What are you doing? Walk across India? Are you [expletive] crazy?*

I know little about India, most of it bad: too many people; bad water and food; poverty; filth. Of course I had planned to go there to see about this Meher Baba, but walk 2,000 miles with camping gear? That is an entirely different matter: crazy, impossible, dangerous, and scary.

Once again I find myself in the back seat of a taxi going to the airport, the passing scenery reminding me how much I love this island paradise that I'm leaving behind. And yes, Duke Ellington is playing. *Love big band.*

Oil portrait of Meher Baba, London, 1931, by Kathy House.
Photo © Robyn House, used by permission.

Chapter Thirteen

Australia

*My desire for knowledge is intermittent; but my desire to commune
with the spirit of the universe, to be intoxicated with the fumes,
call it, of that divine nectar, to bear my head through atmospheres
and over heights unknown to my feet, is perennial and constant.*
—Henry David Thoreau

July, 1981

"Bulla, bulla," exclaims the tall Fijian fellow with a huge smile.

"Bulla, bulla," I reply, feeling a bit silly about it. He is dressed
in a colorful sarong, wearing a headscarf and sandals. He is taller
by two inches than I and has no difficulty handling my satchel,

suitcase, and rolled-up prayer rug. On this, my first visit to Fiji, I have chosen the touristy resort on Nandi for lodging because of the fire-walk that is held there one evening a week.

I'm generally an indifferent tourist, preferring to avoid attractions and sightseeing, but the fire-walk grabbed my attention. Subtle energy? White magic? It seems unlikely that generations of firewalkers could have hoodwinked generations of tourists—it must be real on some level.

Down the slope from the hotel I can see preparations being made, a blazing fire set some two hours before the event. I approach the tall native man of advanced years who is shouting orders to about a dozen younger men, all of them wearing sarongs, their naked torsos glistening with sweat.

"I am the chief," he says in surprisingly good English, extending his oversized hand. I allow that I am an American with great interest in such things.

"How does it work?" I ask.

He shrugs and yells some further instructions to the men who are tending the fire burning over the laid-out stones. The chief then turns to me and replies, "It is only on our island of Beqa that some few men are born with this gift. *The stones don't burn them.*"

"Do they have to go into a trance or practice some ritual?" I ask.

"No, it is a natural gift," he replies. "They will only be burned if they drink alcohol or do sex within three days of a walk."

"Do they have other gifts?" I ask. The chief laughs at the idea and says that I will have to ask their wives. The chief then points to a chair in the front row of seats and says it will be mine when the walk begins.

The evening sky is beginning to color with red and purple, high clouds extending to the horizon. The humid air is warm and close as we make our way to the fire pit. True to his word, the chief escorts me personally to the chair in the front row. The young native men are off to the side of the pit lounging on the ground, animated conversation reaching our ears as they laugh and joke. They clearly aren't meditating.

At the chief's command, they use long palm fronds to sweep the large rocks clear of wood and ash. The exposed rocks are white hot, the pit six feet across and perhaps 20 feet long. Those of us in the front row are sweating freely with the intense heat even as we sit a good distance away. There certainly isn't any trickery here.

At another command, the men form a line and one at a time begin walking barefoot across the stones. Their walk is brisk, but not a running pace at all. Surely, human feet will be instantly scorched with first contact with the stones. Each man completes the walk without incident, our amazement growing. The chief then follows the men across the white-hot stones and, at midpoint, stops and turns to wave at me, smiling his toothless smile before he completes the walk.

There is considerable comment among us as this event concludes; it is truly hard to believe. I and a few others wander over to the men who clearly expect such a thing. Yes, their feet are entirely normal: no calluses, no burns, not even hot to the touch. They laugh at our consternation.

As I walk up the hill alone, I reflect on the huge lesson herein: true, I have personally experienced magical events—many of them—but I suppose that I still have lingering doubts about the status of my mental functioning. However, right here in Fiji is proof positive that such things do exist. I had actually purchased a ticket to watch *magic* unfold in the dusky tropical evening. What other such events are to come? It is an exciting thought to entertain as I make my way to Australia, a five-hour plane ride away.

Maroochydore, a quaint resort town on the east coast of Australia, is surrounded by fields of sugarcane with nearby hills terraced with plantings of spiky pineapples. A wide and slow-moving river soon appears on the left, a sizable mid-river island and walking bridge going out to it. There are huge long-necked pelicans swimming in lazy groups looking more like odd swans than the pelicans we see in America. The island beaches display families on holiday with children playing in the sand, the entire scene a peaceful one and very inviting indeed.

The town soon appears on the right, clapboard cottages and motels here and there, one of which is the Wun Palm Motel, where the driver drops me off. Bill Le Page had booked a room for me and promised to meet me there the next morning. True to name, there is one palm tree in front, an Aussie joke it appears, perhaps the playful work of the owners, a solicitous couple who run the place with cheerful efficiency.

I am bushed and soon fall fast asleep on the narrow bed in the spartan room of the Wun Palm.

As promised, Bill Le Page arrives the next morning. He's a really tall fellow of perhaps 60 years, with silvery hair and bushy eyebrows. He's thin and extroverted with cheerful enthusiasm about everything. "So, you've come to stay with us at Avatar's Abode for a bit," he says after I introduce myself. A momentary cloud passes over his fluid features as he then says, "In Australia, we don't use nicknames at first; you'd best use the name Richard while here." And so it is that I've been Richard ever since.

Bill rushes me over to his Toyota Land Cruiser—Bill always rushes—and we tear through town to Kiel Mountain Road. The two-lane road curves through pineapple fields to the base of the mountain and thence to a steep climb. "We call this hill the pinch," he says, as the engine strains to the top.

Homes soon appear to the right and left, modest ones that are mostly owned, he says, by Baba lovers, the term used for those who believe that Meher Baba—the Ancient One—is love personified. As Bill relates this, I have the uncomfortable feeling that I am being ushered into a cult of some sort. Sweat starts sprouting from my troubled brow. Bill somehow senses this and turns from his driving. "Don't worry, Richard. You'll soon see." As he says these words, I notice that he is wearing Birkenstocks, the first I've seen on anyone else. I can't tell you how reassuring this is. I immediately relax and mentally thank my newly recognized captain for his thoughtfulness.

Diana, Bill's wife, also wears Birkenstocks when I meet her in their home atop the hill. Petite and well matched to Bill's upbeat personality, Diana eventually announces that she hailed from Pasadena, and even more astounding, had been married to Don Succup, the physicist who dropped dead during his AA pitch. Moreover, she knew my friend Bill S., who had finished the dead man's talk after they carted the body away. It was Bill who first gave me Meher Baba's name. All these synchronicities flying about make me feel dizzy and grateful at the same time. My doubts and fears scoot away like a surprised porcupine in the woods.

We sit on barstools in the kitchen as Bill prepares English style tea with milk and sugar. "You're the first Yankee that we've had here, Richard," he says as he hands me a mug of tea.

"Other than me," Diana chimes in with a smile.

"How long are you staying?" Bill asks.

"About three months. I'm leaving for India September 10th."

Bill raises his bushy eyebrows at this. "Amazing, Richard. Diana and I and some others are leaving for India September 9th. Good timing, it seems to me." He slaps me on the back and suggests that we walk up the hill to my quarters, which he warns are modest.

Bill chats amicably as we walk along a dirt path just below the hill where the main buildings of Avatar's Abode are located. Near the tractor barn is a tin shed that serves as rustic accommodation for overnight guests: a bathroom, hot plate, sink, and two bunk beds. "Oh, this will be fine for me, Bill. Thanks." I say.

"Well, it does need some tidying," he says, alluding to the mud that has come in through a space where the tin siding is just shy of the concrete floor. It is through this space, too, that the current occupants have entered—spiders, who have taken up residence in various spots, including the metal supports of the bunk beds. It is thus that I come face to face with the need to conquer a lifelong fear of them, no doubt occasioned by an unwanted contact with a hairy tarantula when I was young.

After a mental shiver, I join Bill outside in the tropical sun and torpid air.

We come upon a metal-clad building that is partially obscured by a large plumeria tree in fragrant bloom. To the other side of the porch is a fenced-in rose garden, quite an attraction for the local wallabies (small kangaroos), Bill says. The building houses a meeting hall with tiered bleachers facing a raised stage. At the rear of the stage is a doorway leading to Baba's room, where he stayed for a few days in 1956 and again in 1958. Bill points to the door. "Okay, Richard. Go on in there and take darshan."

"What does that mean?"

"It means that Meher Baba's presence remains in the room, a connection to his aware state in the beyond. You'll see soon enough."

With those words, Bill leaves to pursue his own daily tasks and promises a tour of the property later that day. *Okay*, I think, *let's see about this.* I open the door.

There is a soft light in the room coming from a window on the opposite wall. Below the window is a narrow bed with a pair of Baba's sandals resting on it. A vase of flowers sits up on the window ledge. Roses. The entire room is paneled in oil-rubbed Australian hardwood, and I notice a worn carpet on the wooden floor.

The visual impact of the room is overpowered by a fragrance, a lilting fragrance that is almost floral but vastly more intriguing than any describable floral essence. I later asked Reg Paffel, one of the men who built the room, about the source of the fragrance. "We don't know. I believe it is divine," he says with a knowing smile.

The entrancing smell that fills my nostrils and the visual impressions pale in comparison to the feeling I experience after stepping into the room. Without conscious thought, I prostrate myself on the worn carpet with my fingertips touching the base of Baba's bed...and I sob with the exquisite emotions of relief, sadness, and joy that gush up from somewhere deep within. I cry with tears and wrenching spasms of a joyful heart that can only be described as *love*, love beyond anything I've ever felt before or since. It goes on and on, until my humanness had bled out and the divine essence within that room has filled the emptiness of separation, filled in the cracks of loneliness and longing until my cup is brimming full. I rise to my knees and sit before this simple bed, breathing in and out, alive in ways I didn't think possible.

Yes, Bill, now I know.

Outside the building I stand on the crest of the hill that slopes down to a deep valley and distant sugarcane fields, rainforest, and scattered homes. Almost to the horizon, I can see the blue waters of the Pacific, the entire vista an idyllic view of beautiful Queensland. Standing there I am also buffeted by surges of dimensional power that radiate outward from that special room I'd just left. I imagine myself levitating upward to the brilliant white clouds and into the arms of angels.

Bill soon appears, forcing me to come back to Earth. I don't like it much, but I gather my thoughts as much as possible and ask about the bird calls that I'd been hearing, not wanting to discuss the wonders that I've just experienced in Baba's room.

"Yes, the kookaburras are the ones that you are hearing now." The small flock is down the grassy slope, their spooky laughter echoing off the hill to the right of the common, a chorus of sound that makes us speak louder.

"Baba's mandali stayed here," Bill says as we approached the other small building on the hill. Mostly, Avatar's Abode is 500 acres of natural habitat with a grassy common and the homes of a few privileged families staying on the hill itself.

In the absence of kookaburra cries, I hear the three-tone whistle that I had first mistaken as human in origin, an assumption that Bill then corrects. "Butcher birds, Richard. They will fly in an open window and steal meat off the counter, hence their name. They picked up their whistle song from early pioneers and carry it forward with each bird generation."

We amble down the path a bit farther and Bill points up the hill to a wooded area. "Francis Brabazon, Baba's dear poet, lives in a cabin up there. He and I were the ones charged by Baba to buy and develop this property for his Australian center. Francis lived in India with Baba for 17 years, but he's an old man now and doesn't see people."

A colorful flock of noisy parakeets settle into the gum trees overhead. Bill and I can scarcely hear each other and walk back to his truck in silence. Because we are quite a distance from the nearest store, Bill offers to take me to a grocery to get basic supplies in Maroochydore. On the way back, I am much more relaxed in his company as the car engine once again strains going up the pinch. Bill drops me off at my quarters and bids me good day.

I ask Bill about a wash bucket and broom and soon start in on the tin shed. Mysteriously, the spiders are all gone, but their cobwebs are still very much in evidence. I brush, sweep, and mop my way into the afternoon until the tin shed is livable. Not enough kitchenware, no contact paper on shelves, and no tea. The next day, I ask Bill for another ride into town.

As we make the steep descent down Kiel Mountain, a sudden thought has me visualizing an arduous walk up it, perhaps with a backpack, the pinch a good training exercise for my walk across India. "Say, Bill, are there any stores in Maroochydore that sell hiking gear?"

"What's this, Richard?"

"Well, I intend to walk across India."

Bill turns to look at me, his usual cheerful demeanor momentarily replaced with incredulity. "Why?"

We've arrived at the marketplace in Maroochydore. I answered Bill's question by relating the high spots of my adventure thus far—that my unseen captain, Meher Baba, has sent the command for me to undertake this journey. We sit in silence for a bit, then Bill turns to me. "I'm glad that Baba has taken you under his wing, but I really don't know that walking across India is a reasonable thing."

"Actually, I agree, Bill, but I'm going to do it anyway. Are there any likely stores here?"

There is a long pause as Bill no doubt is struggling with what to say.

"I don't think so, but Brisbane will have a few. You can ride with me next week."

When I awaken the next morning, it is to fever and chills that announce the presence of an internal invader of viral origin. I'm hardly ever sick, and this unwelcome event lays me up in bed for three days—unbeknownst to the kind people on the hill. I am so weak I that I can't eat or leave the bed for more than a trip to the bathroom now and then.

Will I die here in this tin shed? It feels like it certainly, but not to worry, all things good and bad do pass. Finally I best the virus and leave my sickbed none the worse for wear, my immune system no doubt primed and charged for the assaults I would later experience.

That evening there is a program held in the meeting place. It is the first opportunity I have had to get a good look at the people whose devotion to Baba has led them here. It's a convivial group, it turns out, with people of all ages from youngsters to octogenarians, all of whom seem quite ordinary, if not extremely friendly. I am surprised to receive many hugs along with a "Jai Baba" intoned in my ear. This all-purpose greeting/goodbye conveys recognition of Baba's status and a wish for good tidings. I respond with "Jai Baba," and the ritual is complete. This simple thing is about the only ritual allowed by Baba other than the singing of *arti* twice daily at his center in India, and, for a time, at Avatar's Abode.

This evening's program begins with arti, devotional songs in English and Gujarati, sung with true enthusiasm. The master's prayer is also recited, a difficult thing to memorize, I would soon discover. What follows is a series of skits and songs performed with ardor and occasional skill. I sit in the bleachers, absolutely delighted by all that goes on. I love the sense of togetherness, a balm for my self-imposed isolation, a cure for my chronic aloneness. These people would become family, my Australian family, my Jai Baba friends.

After the program, Bernard Bruford invites me to dinner the next evening, his extended family one of the few Baba asked to reside on the property itself, their home a modest one on the hill above the meeting hall. I knock on the door.

I generally feel awkward at such gatherings, particularly being the Yankee doctor on pilgrimage and all the questions that naturally follow. I find these folks to be the exception as the stories about Baba's visits flow one to the next. Bernard, a school teacher with the gift of language, held us (or at least me) spellbound with his description of meeting Baba, the love radiating from this great soul melting Bernard's heart on first contact. Just then, I see a huge spider on the dining room wall, whereupon Joan Bruford jumps up and whacks it dead with a stout blow from a broom. God, what a monster. Six inches across, easily, a harmless fruit-eating spider, I am told. I will have personal contact with one of these huge arachnoids in the shower one day. It, too, went to heaven after doing me the great service of taking away my fear of them—anything smaller being of no consequence at all.

The remainder of the evening goes well, and I enjoy the temporary release from solitary confinement in my tin shed.

As I get to know these people and hear many amazing stories of lives upended by Meher Baba's call, I am surprised that no one has experienced *magical things* as I had many times over. I had expected to encounter a cadre of similar souls conscripted by the Ancient One along the same lines as I. But no, their stories are amazing in detail, their love profound, but there are no tales of trips to the beautiful land or of car doors that melted away. Also, there are no recovering alcoholics among them, wine and beer freely flowing at gatherings, and no stories of heroic transcendence of impossible circumstance. In this regard, I am surprised and perhaps elated—a certain ratification that my sense of mission is indeed unique—but it brings with it the corresponding feeling of ongoing isolation: I am on my own, me and the captain. Would I get superpowers?

It turns out that the question isn't entirely frivolous.

Reg Paffel, probably in his 70s, an intense and loving Englishman, had been a Sufi under Inayat Khan before he and Francis Brabazon recognized Baba as the avatar. Reg was one of the men who helped Francis develop Avatar's Abode in the early 1950s before Baba's first visit. A horseman, he kept two saddle horses on the property. His first question to me is, "Do you ride?" My answer has us saddling up for a trail ride that afternoon.

I find that my big American feet won't slide into the stirrups all the way, the Australian saddle an odd combination of Western and English style gear. *Never mind*, I think, and we get on with it. The creaking leather and beautiful scenery of the gum forest and rolling hills soon put me in that gracious space of man and horse, and I relax. A disturbance in the bush behind us soon becomes a barking dog, the Le Page's German shepherd, Duke, who nips at my horse's hooves. This creates a great deal of bucking horse upset with me holding on for dear life. Reg starts yelling at Duke, who eventually takes off for other canine adventures in the woods. Reg then hands me a compliment that I've retained all these years: "Nice job at keeping your seat."

Reg and I become good friends as I help him with his chores on the property. Today's task, mixing and pouring concrete for the horse stall floors, is completed to our mutual satisfaction, and at dusk I decide to return for a final check on the curing concrete. The sky is vibrant with color as the setting sun paints the clouds in hues of violet and pink, a glorious end to the day.

"These stalls look like meditation cells," says a strong voice behind me. Startled, I spin around to see a wizened old man, whom I guess to be Francis Brabazon, standing a few feet behind me. As our eyes lock, I realize that his forceful words imply some knowledge of my program even though I haven't discussed any of it with my new Aussie friends. Before I can mount a reply, he continues, looking me straight in the eye. "You can stay here as a yogi, or move on." With that, he turns and silently walks back into the woods.

I had not previously met Francis and was a little frightened of him by report. His many years in India with Baba afforded him high status as a mandali member even as he was a humble soul and gifted poet. I'm standing in front of the *meditation cells*. How did he know about that? I had been quiet about my meditation practice because no one I had encountered thus far was a meditator. Baba mentioned meditation in *Discourses*, but it wasn't an important facet of Baba life among his current followers.

A yogi? I know nothing about yoga or yogis and thus don't fully understand this choice. Not that it matters much; I am truly set on my course and even the offer of superpowers, had I understood it, could not have interrupted my journey, thank you very much.

The cryptic message from Francis and my general earnestness leave me restless and impatient to get on with the main program: what should I do during this Australian prelude?

Initially, I make myself useful, helping Bill with his projects, planting trees, clearing garden beds, and doing general maintenance. I ride with him to property auctions whenever lots contiguous with Avatar's Abode came up for sale. These sorts of activities help to get my feet back on the ground. I set up a bank account in Maroochydore to allow posted funds to arrive from my old practice, as well as monthly payments from the sale of my Porsche. Based on my itinerary, I am able to use American Express offices for the same purpose as I later travel around the globe.

Bill is business-oriented and had done quite well with an import venture in Brisbane. He was originally a psychologist, until Baba admonished him to give up his profession in order to manage the affairs of Avatar's Abode. Baba also instructed Bill to take one ounce of whisky every evening, never explaining the why of it.

Tagging along, I walk the streets of Brisbane in search of camping gear, gradually acquiring the necessities as they present themselves. A mountaineering shop affords the basics: an American Lowe backpack, tent, down-filled sleeping bag, and, most important, a pair of leather bush-walking boots in size 13. Most Aussies have smaller feet, I am told; this pair in size 13 is an anomaly on the back shelf.

The salesman helping me is curious about my plans. "I'm walking across India," I reply.

"Right, then," he says with surprised enthusiasm. "What other treks have you made?" When I admit that it would be my first serious hike, my experience limited to Eaton Canyon in Sierra Madre, he stops calculating the bill and stares at me.

"Right, then," he repeats with a certain note conveying, *This one is crazy, but I'll take his cash and wish him well.* Which he does.

The blisters on both heels are nasty reminders that I've been wearing flip-flops or Birkenstocks for too long; nonetheless, my walks about the property gradually toughen my tender skin to the point that I start serious training. It is warm enough to wear khaki shorts, a blue shirt, and a red headscarf as my basic uniform. I don the Lowe backpack with some trepidation; *Let's start by stuffing it with a pillow and see how it goes.* Adding a bottle of water and some Band-Aids, I set off from my quarters on a bright Australian spring morning. Several of the people along Meher Road wave or shout a greeting as I walk by. Soon I would become *the crazy Yank walking to Nambour—there he goes again.*

That first walk back up the pinch has me huffing and puffing to the extent that I have to stop three times with hands on knees, gasping for breath before I make it to the top. Thankfully, no cars drive by—there are no witnesses to this tenderfoot display of weak flesh.

Undaunted, I repeat the walk the next morning but turn right at the highway and keep on walking. A week later, I thusly make it to Nambour, a town with narrow-gage rails going down Main Street to accommodate the frequent trains of sugarcane on their way to the mill. This day, the clickety-clack reaches my ears as I sit with a cup of tea at a sidewalk café. The families passing by, this a Saturday, remind me of the well-behaved 1950s in America. There goes Dad with a broad-brimmed hat, Mom with a shirtwaist dress, kids in shorts and long socks, no yelling for this or that. The more time I spend in Australia, the more I wonder about the state of affairs in our own country. *It can be like this*, I think, *but probably never will be.*

As the weeks go by, the pillow in my pack is replaced with heavier loads, water on the way out and food items on the return.

Eventually, I tame the pinch and can scale it in one go. *I thought I could. I thought I could...*40-pound pack and all.

During this period, I start and end each day in Baba's room, sitting on the worn carpet while inhaling the perfume of God. These meditations bring in surges of power that sometimes move my head side to side, but never is it thrown back like before. Along with the intense physical conditioning, the meditation sessions seem to energize internal centers that I would later call chakras. It is truly the first time in my life that I feel centered and powerful. India? Why stop at India? Maybe I'll walk the world.

There are occasional evening gatherings at the homes of Baba folks along Meher Road—finger food, beer, and wine—and during them, I am regaled with stories of India, the sweetness of experiencing Baba's tomb-samadhi, his loving presence intensely felt by most. Meher Baba had ordered his tomb excavated years before he left his body there. He sat in the excavated pit for six months, on and off, doing higher-dimensional work. At the conclusion of this phase, he announced that each and every soul who found their way to this place would receive a spiritual boost. After what I had experienced in his room at Avatar's Abode, I can easily believe it.

The other stories that reach my ears are of the great difficulties encountered in India: the throngs of people everywhere, bandits, filth, the perils of travel, the contaminated water and danger of illness from eating and drinking in restaurants unless they are four-star affairs. And I want to spend a year walking across this devil's playground? Yes.

At one such gathering, Francis Brabazon surprises me once again, first by being there at all, and second, by coming up to me with two glasses of wine. Without a word, he hands me one to raise with him as a toast: *"Jai Baba."* As I hold the glass of wine in my hand, my mind buzzes with alarm: *danger, danger, just one drink may kill you,* says my mind. The entire basis of sober living in AA is to not take that first drink ever, ever, ever.

"Jai Baba," I say with enthusiasm and drink the wine. Then the familiar buzz of mild euphoria comes, along with the certainty that I have done the right thing.

(As an aside, I drank wine and beer on and off for two years before resuming total abstinence throughout the past 30 years.)

That evening as we toast Meher Baba, Francis gives me a sly wink; then this wise little man walks off in silence.

The time is approaching to bring India to the forefront; I need shots—inoculations against the microscopic creatures that transmit dysentery, yellow fever, malaria, dengue, and God knows what else. As I am walking to Nambour with this in mind, I notice something very odd. With each cadenced step, I'm mentally repeating a phrase, one word at a time, *no-thanks-very-much-no-thanks-very-much,* over and over. Mind, as we all know, is a big, complicated, human arena with all sorts of things going on at once. The part of my mind that is repeating this phrase is a small part of the total action, so I don't give it much *thought.* Soon, the distractions of the noisy town make me forget about it entirely.

The doctor's waiting room is utilitarian and solemn. There are several people awaiting their turn—trying to avoid staring at the Yank with a full beard and long hair, an oversized backpack by his oversized feet.

I am finally admitted. The tall English doctor with white hair, a trimmed mustache, and rimless eyeglasses is wearing khaki shorts and knee-high socks. A pith helmet would have completed the picture of a colonial M.D. banished to a small town in Queensland, Australia. He has in fact been to India, he says, as he prepares the various inoculations.

"So, how long do you plan on being there?"

"A year if it turns out well; maybe longer," I say with enthusiasm.

"Hepatitis," he says. "That's what a traveler can expect after a time. You must be exceedingly careful. Never eat from street vendors. No ice. No milk, unless it's boiled."

"Thanks very much," I reply as sweat breaks out on my brow.

"No charge," he says as I pull up my drawers. "Good luck, son, and do be careful."

Hepatitis? That's the last thing I need after the huge insult my liver endured during my drinking career, and here I am drinking wine again? *Captain, O captain, are you sure about this?* The immediate answer comes forth as my right hand jumps up with forefinger and thumb forming a circle, a universal *okay* sign that Baba often used. *Okay, okay, let's get on with it.*

The doctor's visit is not only alarming, but it also adds an extra mile to my journey home. The trudge up the incline outside of Nambour finds me dispirited and anxious. Am I crazy? My logical mind insists that I look back to the very beginning of this wild adventure—all of it based on a Maui window decal, and here I am walking up a goddamn hill with a 40-pound pack and a sore butt from inoculations against deadly diseases. And my home is a tin shed...filled with spiders. I must be crazy.

I am startled out of this unpleasant reverie by a familiar sound that I haven't heard in quite some time: the revving sound of an MG engine. I had owned two MGs during my college years, these English sports cars quite distinctive in many ways, but not very practical for everyday use. The throaty sound snaps my head up as I approach a petrol station on the right side of the highway. Yes, a black MG just like the one I once owned is now a few feet away. The woman driving it, I discover, is the most beautiful woman I've ever seen or ever will see—large dark eyes, black hair pulled back, fair skin...and she is smiling at me with such radiance that my heart melts into a slush of wonder and bliss. She leans out the window and her smile blasts away all thought.

"Can I give you a lift to the Baba turnoff?" she asks. I stand dumbstruck and unable to think.

"No thanks very much," I hear myself say.

This creature of such amazing beauty then flashes me the okay sign with finger and thumb, and roars away in her little MG. "Well, okay then," I say aloud as I watch the car disappear over the horizon.

My steps now are swift and sure, the backpack light as a feather. My feet hurry me to the Baba turnoff, *Thank you my angelic friend, thank you.*

Francis sends word that I am to join him for a supper of vegetable soup this evening at precisely 5 o'clock. *What now?* It is September 8, 1981. I am leaving for India in two days. I wait in the woods near his small cabin until my wristwatch announces the appointed hour. Francis Brabazon opens the door, looks up at me and says, "You're right on time. Sit." I do, and I watch while Francis adds a few spices to the boiling pot of soup, the aroma and steam filling his small cabin with olfactory delight. He serves up the soup with slices of bread and we slurp and eat with gusto.

I am at a loss to fully understand this encounter or to come up with anything to say during it; this my first experience with gifts that are given and received in silence. It is only later that I come to realize that I have been graced with the blessing of a great soul— for Francis's soul is such—in preparation for the difficult journey ahead.

Chapter Fourteen

India

*Have patience, candidate, as one who fears
no failure, courts no success.
Fix thy soul's gaze upon the star whose ray thou art.*
—Ancient Buddhist writing

The tin shed has been my home for so long that it is an emotional tussle to leave it, spiders and all. The entire constellation of Australian life coupled with the warm friendships that I'd cultivated, not to forget Baba's special room, prompts a resolution to return one day, perhaps permanently.

Bill Le Page drops me off at the small airport in Maroochydore for the first leg of a journey that 20-some hours later will find me in India, disheveled, tired, and excited.

The Santa Cruz International Airport in Bombay (Mumbai) is not, to my great surprise, air-conditioned. The hot, sticky air grows mold on the concrete walls of the customs area where I stand in a queue behind an Arab family who, along with several children and two trolleys of luggage, are carrying a mattress into India—with good reason, I would later discover.

My own trolley is overburdened with a suitcase, my 60-pound backpack full of camping gear, antibiotics, and various medicines, plus my rolled-up prayer rug. I had purchased the medicines and a fair supply of cutlery as potential gifts for Mother Teresa. I explain this to the customs man, who goes through each and every item under the watchful eye of a superior making comments in Hindi.

I begin to despair ever entering the country. They unroll the prayer rug, which seems to bother them the most.

"No, I'm not a Muslim," I reply. "Yes, it's from Iran, but I bought it in Pasadena." Finally, the fellow stamps my passport and his superior walks away. I wipe the sweat from my brow and join the noisy throng outside in the humid night air of India.

The tumult is unbelievable. It's still quite dark, the air so sultry that it feels like ocean and air combined. The olfactory portion of my brain snaps awake: such smells—exotic Indian breath laden with spice and the dense aromas of humanity that swirl around in my brain looking for context. There is none, all of it unique and all of it enlivening, this smell of India.

Young boys swarm around me like buzzing bees, entreating, pleading with upturned faces and large black eyes. "Come, come with me, mister." I resist and power through the crowd toward a line of black taxis that snakes far into the distance, the lead taxi summoned by an armed guard on request. Bill had advised me to do just that, but a young boy manages to wrest my suitcase from me before I can get there, and I am soon trotting after him with worried alarm. "Follow me, mister," he keeps repeating, until we arrive at a small car manned by his uncle. I know enough to accede to providence, and soon am negotiating the fare with the driver according to guidelines supplied by Bill.

"Okay, okay, get in," and we are off to the Dadar taxi stand across Bombay. The next sensory assault is the noise, the sound of the driver honking his horn every few seconds, along with other drivers doing the same, seemingly as a reflex rather than based on traffic conditions. The smell of diesel fumes and honking horns soon drift into my consciousness as permanent impressions of travel in India. The smell of diesel fumes...I'm just tired enough that my mind drifts back to that distant day when I walked behind Father through the rows of orange trees, the smudge pots radiating heat and billowing black smoke. Here I am once again, following my unseen captain...Meher Baba.

The young Indian boy sitting next to his uncle in the front seat rouses me out of this pleasant reverie. "Where you from, mister?"

I smile at him before replying, "I don't know."

Six bumpy hours and two taxi stands later I arrive at the Pune taxi stand. Now an experienced taxi traveler with a sore butt, I buy all the seats in this taxi, which is soon to depart for Ahmednagar. I notice several other Westerners wandering about, Rajneesh followers I would later learn. His ashram in Pune had gained considerable notoriety because of this dubious Indian master's promise of easy enlightenment. Rajneesh advised his followers to indulge their lower instincts—sex, drugs, alcohol—to rid these vices from the psyche. This simplistic philosophy with tantric overtones was seductive, but it offended Indian sensibilities to the point that Rajneesh moved his operation to Oregon, attracting many intelligent, well-meaning Americans until it all collapsed due to unsavory activities there as well.

The Meher Baba Trust compound is a welcome oasis, a court-yard with several offices and small domiciles along gated walls. The taxi-walla has quite a time finding it, which adds some anxious moments to this last stage of the journey, and once there, I almost collapse in gratitude.

"Welcome, Richard. We've been expecting you," says Pat Summer, an Aussie who had been living in India for years. "What's all this?" she asks, taking in my surfeit of luggage.

"Ah, it's camping gear," I say without explanation, "and a prayer rug."

"Right." Pat registers me with the local police, a necessary pro-cedure because of problems encountered with the Rajneeshees in Pune. "No worries, Richard, you're set. I'll call up a rickshaw to take you to the Pilgrim Center. Your camping gear will stay here in the lockbox."

I nod. Pat and I would become good friends over the years, though this first meeting is somewhat strained. *Camping gear? This is a place for prayer and meditation, not recreation. Camping in India? This Yank is clearly crazy.*

Riding in a motorized rickshaw is a worthy experience, one that I look back on with great fondness. It's noisy, smelly, jolting, and even dangerous, but I love this form of transport more than any other. The owners/drivers of same tend to be intelligent, in-formed, and quite willing to supply the traveler with whatever, and go wherever—just ask—and be willing to negotiate.

The town of Meherabad had been acquired for Meher Baba's work in the 1920s. At the time, there was an old post office building and water tank room on a sloping hill above the railroad and high-way, and a few disused buildings on the other side of the road: lower Meherabad.

When I arrive on September 12, 1981, I am amazed as the rickshaw pulls up to the newly completed Pilgrim Center, a large one-story building that looks like a Spanish villa with tiled roof and arched front porticos, the stonework and architecture unlike anything I've seen in India. I will learn that it had been designed and built by an American architect (and Baba lover), Ted Judson. It is a refreshing sight and speaks of comfort and security as I lug my suitcase up the stone steps to the shady porch. There are a few Westerners sitting there, one of whom directs me to a small office down the hallway. Inside, I meet Gary Kleiner, who sits back in his chair with hands clasped behind his head.

"So, you're Richard," he says simply. "From?"

"California, I guess, but I've been traveling. And you?" I ask, taking in his accent.

"Chicago, but this is home now." He reaches over to give me a lock and key. "So, do you play volleyball? Game's tomorrow at three."

My room is small, a bed with mosquito netting, a desk, and a lockable closet framed in aged teakwood from a dismantled Buddhist monastery. A window above the desk looks out to the hallway and the supporting stone arches that circle the open central courtyard. The bathroom down the hall features both Eastern and Western toilets and stalls for the bucket baths allowed every third day. *Every third day?*

After unpacking and stowing my suitcase, I walk around the stone hallway to the opposite side of the courtyard. Delectable smells of cooking come from the kitchen, where I meet Alan Wagner, an American whose promise to all pilgrims is to provide safe, nourishing fare in the dining room. His culinary skills, I would soon discover, are matched only by his theatrical abilities and operatic voice.

Bushed, I return to my room and flop on the bed, the honking horns of the nearby road a sweet lullaby as I sink into a dreamless sleep.

Kleiner is still in his office, still with hands clasped behind his head, when I awaken in late afternoon,

"So, Richard, you're going up to Samadhi?"

I nod. "What do I do up there?"

"Well, nothing really. There are no rules. Most people bow at the threshold and then kneel at the marble slab for a few moments. That's it. You can sit on the mats along the wall after that. When you leave, the watchman will hand you prasad, orange candy usually, a sweet gift from God, so to speak." Kleiner then motions for me to go on. "You'll see."

I walk about 50 yards to the road and again marvel at the utter diversity of noisy travel on it, a moving river of beast and man that I carefully cross without incident. A few yards farther I come to the railroad tracks, no trains in sight, the shiny rails converging to pinpoints as I look right then left before stepping over them.

The gravel path going uphill is bordered by young trees every 20 feet or so, the sun not yet deflected by them. At the top of the hill to the right I see the compound wall around the old tank room, and next to the gate, dead ahead, a small tin shed. To the left is Baba's tomb-samadhi, a mortared stone building with a white dome atop it, symbols of the major religions along its perimeter: Christian, Jewish, Muslim, Hindu, Buddhist, and Zoroastrian. There is a shady porch over the entrance to the tomb from whence an old man is coming toward me. It is Nana Kher, one of Baba's mandali and a permanent resident who often hands out prasad. As we meet, he enfolds me in a tender embrace and whispers in my ear, "Welcome home, son." This exquisite moment wipes away all fear and opens my heart like a love song from God.

There are tombs of revered saints and perfect masters all over India, the idea being that the *presence* of these elevated souls remains at the spot where they are buried, the people visiting, *taking darshan*, accruing spiritual benefit simply by bowing down.

After what I had experienced in Baba's room at Avatar's Abode, I can't imagine what is in store here, at the center of Baba's life on earth, and even more, of course: the place where Baba left his physical remains.

As I bow and enter the tomb, the fragrance of tuber rose, marigold, and jasmine floats the words *welcome home* once again. My mind vanishes altogether, and in those precious moments, I prostrate myself on the stone floor, wrenching sobs from the depths of my heart filling my ears with the sound of sweet surrender, the cool marble on my forehead the touch of divine ease and love. When I raise up and look about in wonder, I see God everywhere: in the mortared stone, in the beams of light from the window, in my hands on my knees, in the photo of smiling Baba, and, *looking inward*, in the very folds of my heart.

I spend many hours in the tomb in the weeks that follow. Each time, the experience is different, but the overall sense is, in two words, LOVE and POWER.

I also spend hours in the tin shed about 20 feet away from where Baba frequently sat in silence. In this small room, I feel POWER and LOVE.

In later years I would understand the metaphysics herein, the tomb a primary energy nexus, and the tin shed a secondary one. There is a vast energetic network all over the world (and universe) that arises from, and is maintained by, primary and secondary energy spots corresponding to *1 and 2*, the organizing principle of all that is—and all that is not.

All humans on Earth have the latent ability to consciously experience the energetic organization that underlies the visible universe. In my case, this ability is just opening, and it is astonishing, to say the least. The tin shed will prove to be the most powerful nexus of mental energy that I would ever encounter. It is the source of all secondary spots on Earth. This original secondary nexus located in the tin shed is a partner to the Om point, the original *primary* nexus that has a physical locus about a hundred miles away from Baba's tomb-samadhi. It is Baba's tomb and his conscious connection to it that modulates the flow between these two partnered spots. It is here that avataric consciousness enters and directs all events in the creation, the home place of Christ consciousness, as it were.

The primary energy spots on Earth are analogous to Ida, in the human chakra system as noted in yogic theory—yin in the Chinese system. The secondary spots on Earth are analogous to Pingala—yang energy in the human body.

Just as human metaphysical anatomy contains energy channels called nadis arising from Ida and Pingala, and spinning energy pumps called chakras, the Earth is covered in similar channels of energy storage and flow in a complex system called the grid, made of ley lines that originate from the Om point as primary channels and spots with corresponding secondary channels and spots all over the earth.

It will take years for me to understand this grand system first glimpsed in the tin shed in 1981 in Meherabad.

Bill and Diana Le Page are staying at Meherazad, Meher Baba's actual home located several miles away, a beautiful compound that is the home of the remaining mandali. It was quite a shock to the people closest to Baba when he dropped his body in 1969. Since that time, the mandali have carried on Baba's various programs of service to the poor while making themselves available to the increasing number of visitors that come to this special place from all over the world.

Several other Aussies are staying with me at the Pilgrim Center, all good friends by now, and a busload of us is about to depart for Meherazad to visit the handful of mandali that still live. My seat-mate, Richard Lockwood, regales me with his life story as the bus bumps along the dusty road to Meherazad. Richard had been the lead singer of a popular Australian rock and roll band until a mystical experience so changed his life that he now drives a taxi in Sydney and sings songs to God, not man.

Richard pauses and turns to me. "What's your story, then?" This question has come up several times before, giving me reason to concoct a truthful story that didn't admit to the magical or frankly unbelievable; I keep quiet about these things, a course that I would follow for many years afterward. Wouldn't you?

Several of the mandali meet the bus as we pull into the courtyard. Ordinary-looking Indian men and women of advanced age, they are nonetheless dazzling—as if illuminated by bright sunlight even though the sun is hiding behind a cloud. The brightest of all is Mani, Baba's sister. Her wide dark eyes and silvery hair gleam with something that is beyond description...perhaps light, but not just that. Moreover, she prances and dances about, a delightful imp, giving smiles and hugs to us all, one by one. When my turn comes, she looks me in the eye and pulls me close, whispering in my ear, "We've been waiting for you." Then off she goes to another. I am stunned, to say the least. *How could she know? What did she know? What does it mean?* I have little remaining interest in meeting the other mandala, and at the first opportunity I walk up the hill behind Meherazad where the shock of that precious message from Mani is carried off on the breeze of wonderment.

On subsequent visits, I do meet the other mandali and also sit listening to Eruch, one of Meher Baba's closest mandali, tell stories in Mandali Hall, as do the others. I notice no special attention from the mandali and expect none. This is private business. This is between my captain and me, I a covert operative on a secret mission—or so it seems. There is a part of me that understands all this and another part that declares it fanciful thought in the extreme. I have to rely on something far removed from pure logic to make peace with it all, and I feel certain that my upcoming walk across India will open my eyes to the truth of the matter. I have a destination now, the precise location for my appointment with destiny: Calcutta.

One afternoon after visiting Meherazad, I get off the bus at the Trust Office in Ahmednagar with the idea of doing a little shopping. This was born from a conversation with Dan Ladinsky, a fellow pilgrim and accomplished poet who has traveled extensively in India. "You need to be careful, Richard. There are *dacoits* (bandits) that prey on Westerners. You need to watch where you're going and keep a low profile." It is this last piece of advice that has me shopping for burlap to cover my brightly colored Lowe backpack.

Ahmednagar is a bustling town with the usual conglomeration of people and their various modes of transport that jam all the roads all the time. Plus, there are lop-eared goats and the occasional sacred cow wandering among them while mangy dogs warily roam about as well, the entire spectacle much like a state fair in America with sidewalk vendors hawking their wares, noisy commerce and motion everywhere.

The shops themselves are open air, the shopkeepers often sitting cross-legged on elevated platforms along with their goods— dry foods, spices, hardware, or perhaps crockery, a mishmash of goods for sale at negotiable prices.

I wind my way through the crowds but am unable to find burlap or a lock and key for my journey—lesser hotel rooms offering a hasp but no lock, I was told. Back at the Trust Office I ask around for Jimmie, a reliable rickshaw driver, and the two of us get it done together, both vendors I need located in alleys where I wouldn't have dared to venture on my own.

❦

There are about 50 of us Westerners staying at the Pilgrim Center. Because many of them had not known much about Meher Baba beforehand, films are often shown in the evenings. On this sultry night, the movie is not only the first that I have seen of Baba, with his incredibly graceful movements, but is also one of the most notable ever filmed. In 1941, Meher Baba had arranged for an unusual meeting with one of the five living perfect masters, Upasni Maharaj, who, along with the other four, was responsible for Baba being on Earth.

Five perfect masters are always on Earth serving as direct agents of God's will—a fact that has gone unrecognized in Western Culture. I have heard it said that the Three Wise Men of biblical lore were in fact perfect masters, giving their spiritual gifts to the Christ child. Perfect masters are souls that have experienced the complete journey of evolution of form from the gaseous states to fully evolved human. Then, having achieved perfection throughout countless lifetimes on Earth and having traversed the final pathway to God on the subtle and mental planes of the spiritual path, they are united with eternal existence. Instead of remaining absorbed in everlasting divine bliss, they reestablish conscious connection with physical forms and their own bodies to serve as man-God on Earth. Some of these souls have been revered as great saints, Sai Baba being an example, with millions of followers in the East, even though he dropped his body in 1918. His photo can be seen all over India and not uncommonly in Indian homes in America. Sai Baba's seat, Shirdi, is in the Ahmednagar district not far from Meherabad.

Upasni Maharaj was destined to be a sadguru also. He sat with Sai Baba, whom Hindus recognized as a powerful sadguru and Muslims also revered as Qutub, a rare convergence of Hindu and Muslim tradition. When Upasni had completed his own journey via the grace of Sai Baba, he took his seat at Sakori nearby. Volumes have been written about these two incomparable souls and their connection to Meher Baba, the avatar or God-man.

One of the most difficult metaphysical concepts for most people to accommodate is that the perfect masters—and the avatar—are each the exact center of the universe. Throughout the ages, these special souls who are one with God have reported seeing the universe emanate from their own being. Upasni Maharaj reported seeing the galaxies of suns and planets issue forth from his abdomen (third chakra). Meher Baba once said that he could see the entire creation stream outward from his heart (fourth chakra).

Although this notion has been bouncing around in my mind, there is no possible frame of reference for it until I watch the film that evening at the Pilgrim Center. Upasni Maharaj, an old man, portly and naked but for a gunnysack loincloth, was pictured meeting Meher Baba in the countryside near Ahmednagar. As they approach each other, it makes me gasp, as I'm powerfully shaken with a vertiginous feeling of *impossibility*: I can see two exact centers of universal energy streaming forth side-by-side, a chaotic clashing coordinance that twists my mind into a wavering knot. I am shocked and transfixed at the same time. Any question that I may have harbored about the true status of Meher Baba is settled in that instant. These matters are beyond mind and don't apply to logic. It is only through direct experience and the opening of faculties beyond mind itself that understanding deeper truths is possible. It is clear to me, as I sit with other Westerners watching the film, that I am seeing it with different eyes than they, and that I will be forever different from them.

After arti the next morning, Gary Kleiner calls out to me as I pass his office on the way to my room. "So, Richard, would you like to join a group of us going to Shirdi and Sakori?"

"Of course," I say, with some wonder at the synchronicity of the event. Kleiner again tries to interest me in a game of volleyball, which I decline with a laugh.

The next morning, six of us climb in the van and make the short trip to the village of Shirdi, the seat chosen by Sai Baba in 1858. This great saint was born to a Brahmin family but was raised by a Muslim saint, a Sufi, who recognized his elevated status. Sai Baba's subsequent life's work as a powerful perfect master has been well documented. In the usual case, when perfect masters complete their Earth-related mission, they pass into universality to experience divine bliss eternally. In contrast, Sai Baba has maintained his conscious link with the creation to help marshal the forces that will usher in the new age, the Age of Aquarius.

After Merwan Irani (Meher Baba), at age 19, had been kissed on the forehead by the ancient woman Qutub, Hazrat Babajan, in 1914, he was absorbed in divine bliss for nine months. Thereafter, he was drawn to Sai Baba in Shirdi who, upon seeing Merwan, called out, *Parvardigar* (the Ancient One) three times. Sai Baba then induced Merwan to visit Upasni Maharaj in Sakori nearby. Upon seeing Merwan, Upasni picked up a stone and threw it with great force, striking Merwan in the center of his forehead. This blow by the hand of a perfected soul brought Merwan's consciousness back to Earth (gross) levels. Upasni then became Meher Baba's guru and teacher.

As the van enters the village of Shirdi, it is clear that the town has been given over to serving the many pilgrims that visit Sai Baba's tomb daily. There are kiosks and shops selling garlands and coconuts for offerings at his entombed feet. People mill around outside with nervous excitement, and incense fills the air. Sai Baba had promised that his followers would continue to receive his *nazar*, his attentive glance, ensuring their basic needs of food and shelter—no small thing in India. No doubt this is in part responsible for the crowds of people who arrive daily to pay homage to this great soul.

Sai Baba's sarcophagus is within a large ornate hall with a waiting area to accommodate pilgrims, where I now sit with Kleiner and the others. When the hall is filled, an odd-looking fellow opens doors to let us march by the tomb and bow down briefly. There is still a small note of Christian hesitation at bowing down when my turn comes. Nonetheless, it is swept away by the palpable aura of *authority*, for want of a better word, that I sense at the tomb. Sai Baba's presence feels like an invincibility similar to that of a seasoned warrior, yet it is comforting and not at all frightening, a welcome sense that someone is in charge and that all is well.

Outside, I wait for the others, listening to the cries of the shop wallas selling souvenirs and bananas. Our small group then heads to Sakori in the van. On the way, we compare Sai Baba experiences, theirs being strikingly similar to my own. I don't think that my sheltered upbringing would have admitted the possibility of a past perfect master still wielding authority on Earth, unless I had experienced it directly.

The short trip to Sakori, also in the Ahmednagar district, brings us to an enclave where Upasni Maharaj had taken his seat. There are tall trees giving shade to a narrow building containing his tomb. It is a low-key affair with none of the boisterous activity we had experienced at Shirdi. Upasni had sat at Sai Baba's feet for the years it took for him to achieve perfection. Upasni had been married three times, outliving his wives, before his duties as sadguru had taken him out of ordinary life. His garrulous nature and powerful charisma attracted only the most devoted seekers of truth. Young Merwan was one such soul who sat in his hut for several years. The stone that Upasni had thrown began the long process of bringing Merwan's consciousness down to Earthly levels after his experience of divine union. Eventually, to the surprise of other devotees, Upasni pronounced Merwan perfect—the avatar of the age, the Ancient One again walking on Earth.

As our group enters the cool building housing Upasni's tomb, we are greeted by a photo of Meher Baba hanging on the wall. We are ushered into the tomb area by Godavi-mai, Upasni's celebrated successor, whom Meher Baba said was almost perfect. The gentle atmosphere as we bow down is in stark contrast to the powerful feel at Shirdi. Each perfect master's personality and attributes is quite different, as their life stories attest. The individual attributes of the five who call down the Ancient One are then combined within the avatar and define the personality and mission of this Christ-conscious soul during and after the advent. Each avatar remains conscious of, and works within, the creation for about one hundred years after leaving his body on Earth.

After we have all paid our respects in the shrine, I sit up front with Kleiner as he drives us back to the center. "So, Richard, what did you think?" he asks.

"I can't believe that we don't know about all this in America," is my response. We both agree that our Christian friends would have a difficult time with these mystical concepts, just as I had: It is a lot to accommodate.

Kleiner asks me about my plans. "Well, I'm leaving on my walk across India in three days."

"Walk across India?" He looks at me with raised eyebrows. Apparently he hadn't understood that my intent was to be on foot as I headed to Calcutta. I explain that I have been charged by my captain, Meher Baba, to go to Calcutta, that I feel certain I will encounter a perfect master there and thus meet my spiritual destiny.

We ride in silence for a bit before he replies, "You should talk to Bhau Kalchuri about your walk. He may have some recommendations for you. I think you have to register with the police in each district on arrival, stuff like that."

Bhau Kalchuri is in charge of pilgrim affairs, but is very busy with his writing of *Lord Meher*, Baba's definitive biography at 6,000 pages. Bhau's fierce countenance is intimidating to me and I am grateful when Kleiner volunteers to arrange the meeting with him and to be my advocate as well.

The next day Kleiner and I are admitted to Bhau's room by John Connor, his ever-present secretary. John, a Westerner who has been serving Bhau in India for years, is tall and thin and looks more like an American lawyer than a factotum for a spiritually advanced Brahmin.

The room is somewhat dark and I can see a glow around Bhau's head. His fiery temperament and presence leaves little doubt about his temporal authority. Bhau sits with his hands clasped over his ample belly. John, who would later become a good friend, stands behind Bhau in respectful silence.

"So, what is this?" Bhau asks Kleiner.

"Well, Richard here, an American, has been touched by Baba's grace." Bhau nods his head without looking at me. I'm starting to feel an upset that increases my heart's tempo, which I can hear beating in my ears.

Kleiner goes on: "He feels that Baba has charged him to make pilgrimage to Calcutta...on foot." Bhau again nods without looking at me. There is dead silence, and in the close air of the room I start sweating. Kleiner recognizes that more needs to be said. "He's been conditioning in Australia for the past three months and has all the gear he needs for the trip."

The silence grows in intensity for a few moments as Bhau stares at Kleiner, and I start to feel panic blistering my mind. Moments pass before Bhau states emphatically, "He can't go. He can't do it."

Kleiner then looks at me as I'm staring at Bhau, searching for some crack in this concrete statement. Kleiner wipes a smudge off the desk in front of us before speaking again. "Richard feels strongly that Baba has asked him to do this thing, and he is prepared to die if it comes to that."

Bhau then leans forward on his desk and replies, "He cannot do it; I won't permit it. He will be killed within a day."

Kleiner looks at me and shrugs. We both stand as John Connor opens the door for us. Outside, Kleiner lightly places his hand on my shoulder. "I'm sorry," he says with true feeling and walks away.

Much like a loose piece of yarn that upon tugging can unravel a knitted sweater, I feel my entire program disintegrating row by row until there is a sorry pile of useless yarn at my feet, leaving me devastated and exposed, naked and shivering in the tropical heat. Of course, Bhau has no real authority to stop me, but I know how these things work. I can't possibly go against his will.

Captain, O Captain, why hast thou forsaken me? As I walk from lower Meherabad I stop at the noisy road, my mind a muddle of confusion and despair. *Have I screwed up?* I notice a momentary gap in the noisy traffic and cross the road, my feet plodding without conscious thought. I come to the railroad tracks and my feet stop me as I stand between the iron rails. My head then snaps to the right and my mind follows the tracks into the distance, until far beyond the horizon I see Calcutta. *I see Calcutta. Oh,* my mind volunteers, *all I need to do is take the train. What an awesome thing!* My heart then zooms into the stratosphere where the air is thin and cool. I hear God laughing, the echoes reaching all the way to Calcutta and then back to where I stand.

Chapter Fifteen

Calcutta

Communion with the transcendent powers...is not a feat that can be achieved by anyone; it is a mystery peculiar to the one elected, and is therefore through and through personal in character.

—Theodore Roszak

O compassionate captain, lead me to my destiny and life's work; I will be pleased to take the train.

I hear a confounding note as destiny's song entices me onward. It is the distant remembrance of that other Richard, the proud doctor who served humanity in other ways—and was well paid for it. What about Megan and Steve and all the others who gave my life definition and stability? How can I walk away from who I was?

I look down at my feet, the ultimate agents of decision-making, and see that they are carrying me back to the Pilgrim Center. I notice that my hands are flexing and quite anxious to start packing for the trip. With a spontaneous chuckle, I admonish my mind to sit back and enjoy the ride.

As I am rolling my prayer rug into burlap and securing it with hemp twine, I stop a moment to consider its purpose. I've lugged it halfway around the world. For what? The answer becomes clear as I inadvertently cut my hand on the rough twine, the blood dripping onto the stone floor of my quarters. Suddenly, I see myself giving the rug to the *perfect master* that I will surely meet in Calcutta— the rug a devotional gift. I will pledge my life to him in service and obedience. My blood will be shed for him, a guardian of the creation. What more worthy cause can there be?

The entire time I've traveled in India, I seem to know what to do and where to go without giving it much conscious thought. I don't sit down and plot out an itinerary—what spots to visit, where to stay, how much it will cost, and so on. So this day I simply heft my 40-pound pack, grab the rug, and take a rickshaw to the S.T. Bus Station in Ahmednagar. Yes, my captain has issued me a rail pass, but there is a place to visit first, it seems: the caves of Ellora and Ajanta near Aurangabad, where Baba occasionally did inner work.

There are seven million people in transit on the roads of India at any given time, many of whom travel by S.T. buses. Similar to American school buses but painted a light blue color with unglassed windows and luggage racks on top, they are everywhere.

The bus station consists of a small ticket office and a large open space where blue buses are randomly parked, some full, some empty, with milling crowds of people around each one. Ticket in hand, I approach the nearest empty bus reciting my litany: "Aurangabad? Aurangabad?"

Various pointed fingers eventually lead me to the proper over-stuffed bus, which is about to depart. I brazen my way forward through the crowd until I reach the open doorway, men standing on the steps within.

"Aurangabad? Aurangabad?" One of the men nods and pulls me aboard, no small feat with my encumbrances. The bus is full of people, all seats taken. I see women in colorful saris and men in various styles of dress standing in the aisle. Soon, amid great commotion, I am propelled down the aisle with difficulty, whereupon two Indian men give up their seats so that I and my gear can plop down. As I do so, the bench seat breaks away from the floor, and the seat and I fall backward onto the two unfortunate passengers behind. There are *oohs* and *aahs* as I wrench the seat forward and, with some rope from my pack, tie it off to the seat in front. *Aha!* says the crowd.

The honking horn announces our departure, and my journey begins.

The hotel in Aurangabad that offers morning trips to the caves is not a four-star affair. It is with some hesitancy that I sit down to dinner in the restaurant, fluorescent lights buzzing above, and I the only customer.

"Dal and rice, please, and bottled water," I request, the same meal I always order while dining in India. Dal, a spicy lentil soup, and steamed rice, as safe as any prepared food can be. Nevertheless, my intuition has proven correct. I am sick all through the night, but not seriously so. It's the only such episode I would suffer during my travels, although I occasionally go hungry as a precaution. After a sleepless night due to gastrointestinal upset, I am still enthusiastic about the day's prospects. The tour bus is idling in front of the hotel as the driver and his helper secure the group's luggage atop the roof. I am the only Westerner, it appears, as I find a seat next to a well-dressed man with graying hair, who greets me with a handshake. I soon learn his name, S.I. Mohile, and that he is a retired lawyer with a spiritual bent who wants to visit the ancient caves as part of a pilgrimage to sacred places in India; this his first stop.

"These caves at Ellora," he says, "go back to the fifth century. Some were carved out by Buddhists and served as monasteries, while others were Hindu and Jain, all existing side by side until the 1800s—amazing to us now."

I nod in agreement, since current religious animosity would hardly permit such familiarity. Meher Baba said that the intense spiritual atmosphere of the place itself and the religious tolerance of the time made it possible for such a thing to occur. "What ended it?" I ask Mr. Mohile.

"No one knows. And why," my friend asks, "are you visiting this place?"

"I've been staying at Meher Baba's ashram, and am traveling across India."

"Ah, I know of Meher Baba, a true saint," he said, a welcome thing for me to hear from an educated man with a spiritual bent.

The caves are located high on a cliff face and require an arduous climb up hundreds of stone steps. It is remarkable to see the many women in their colorful saris slowly make their way upward. The wealthy or infirm hire palanquin to carry them, four young men making a difficult living doing so. S.I. Mohile and I are in good shape and soon make our way up to the cave entrances.

During the climb, I notice that my left hand has assumed a posture of extended index and fifth fingers, with clenched middle fingers—odd. This recalled the spontaneous finger and hand postures I'd experienced in Hawaii, so I'm not overly surprised, just curious.

My lawyer friend and I then enter a large cave with ancient frescoes on the walls and a larger-than-life-sized carved sculpture of reclining Buddha in the center of the room. I am surprised to see that Buddha in all his ancient glory exhibits the exact same posture of his left hand that mine had unconsciously assumed a few moments before. I stand looking down at my left hand in wonder. *What does it mean?* I silently ask the reclining statue. *What does it matter?* the statue replies, laughter echoing off the walls of my mind.

The other caves are interesting and awesome in their functional beauty: ornate Hindu temples coexisting with the simple lingams of Shiva. There are monasteries with sleeping quarters, pillows fashioned from stone, and every manner of artful decoration preserved from ancient days.

What I feel most strongly is the energy of higher dimensions, a gossamer feeling of peace and purpose that leaves me impatiently awaiting new mystical experiences. There are none, even though Mr. Mohile and I spend the day going through many such caves in Ellora and Ajanta.

The train station in Aurangabad is not nearly as frenetic as the bus terminal had been, or perhaps I have just become more accustomed to the scene.

"A first class ticket to Nagpur?" I ask.

"No problem, sir," the clerk says as he waggles his head side-to-side in the typical Indian affirmation. I have decided to buy a ticket to Nagpur, about halfway, instead of through to Calcutta. *One never knows* is my thought at the time.

The train patiently waiting at the platform reminds me of my childhood Lionel train set, the old-fashioned locomotive puffing out black smoke, its baleful whistle somehow exciting and scary. Upon closer examination, I see there are horizontal bars across the unglassed windows of the coaches, giving the appearance of a prison train were it not for the unshackled arms waving from many windows as new passengers, including me, board the rear coaches that are not yet filled to capacity.

The pleasant clickety-clack sound and rolling motion of the train induces a dreamlike state that sends my seatmates to sleep, newspapers on laps, and leaves me adrift in between this world and the next. I remember the passing fields of green plants growing in the harsh soil of India, oxen and implements guided by turbaned farmers dressed in white. I would learn that this common crop is called pulses (lentils), a dietary staple that I would enjoy eating as dal during my travels across this ancient country.

Raipur, where I decide to overnight, is lit up with parades in the street, banging drums and music filling the air. The clerk at the large hotel says that it is a Hindu festival day and that the celebration would continue all night. The sounds of drums and blaring music eventually fade into dreamless sleep.

When I awaken, it is a different hotel and a different city. Groggily alarmed, I shower and dress, noting that my clothes are just this side of filthy. The clerk downstairs affirms that I am in Nagpur, the farthest my purchased train ticket would take me. It is only then that I vaguely recall other hotels and other days on the train. My state of intoxication, so different from one chemically induced, is filigreed with joy and not remorse. My sense of alarm soon shifts to one of urgent prodding from my captain: *no time to lose, no time to lose. Get there.* I take a taxi to the airport, the hell with the train.

The Indian Airlines plane descends into Calcutta in late afternoon. As I disembark, I actually stop on the tarmac and announce to the blue sky above, *Okay, I'm here.*

The stone façade of the New Kenilworth Hotel is reminiscent of the embassies nearby, the central courtyard giving it a grand appearance that makes me wonder about affordability. I resolve to pay the rates, whatever they may be, but am surprised as the matronly woman announces much lower rates than I expected. I quickly sign the register and pay a week in advance, noticing a dining room off to the right with two waiters standing at attention with white linen napkins draped over forearms European style.

The woman keeps my passport, as is the custom in hotels, and advises that my room came with a servant who would bring food and drink upon request.

She claps her hands and the fellow appears, an older man who shoulders my pack and struggles across the courtyard with my suitcase in hand. I carry the prayer rug and hurry behind him as we approach a square stone tower at the opposite end. There is a room below and one at the top of a flight of stairs. The servant, called Jai, stands aside, allowing me to ascend. At the top of the stairs there are tall double doors painted black, *the very same doors that had appeared in my dream in Hawaii, the dream room where my spiritual marriage was to take place.* I actually look down to see if I am magically wearing a tuxedo, but, no, just dirty khakis and scuffed boots.

Jai then unlocks the doors and gives me the key. The interior of the room is dark, just like in the dream, and remains so even when I turn on the floor lamp.

Finally, a place to stay for a while—air conditioned, no less.

Somewhere around 2 a.m., I awaken and look out the window. The hotel is dark, no people in evidence; the place quiet as a tomb. I arise and sit in the chair, the only light coming from the cracked bathroom door. I soon enter the timeless blank of existence where nothing stirs, but where everything awaits expectantly. My head snaps back on my neck, my mouth falls open, and I gasp at the sudden pain, a remembered pain that is insistent but not at all unwelcome. Unlike before, the gurgling pain is tolerable. It carries me to a netherworld where pain is a minor inconvenience. I sit and sit, as the night fades into a surmised dawn as my ears record the sounds of human discourse outside. I peek. The drapes show a lighter color, just as I thought they might. I hear the chittering of birds outside, then the bark of a dog. These sounds of Earth dissolve the netherworld as my neck releases forward and I creak to my feet, each foot a mysterious pad that meets the surface of the concrete floor, each wanting to move in sequence. Then it all floods back: I'm here. My neck hurts like hell. *There is a beautiful land where all your dreams come true...* These lyrics from an Anthony Newley show tune start clearing my mind and refreshing my mood, which is expectant. I massage my neck and walk outside to the panorama of Calcutta. *There is a beautiful land...*

The streets are like arteries and veins, pulsing with ebb and flow, always moving, each person in the crowd intent on some business, either on foot as I am or in the various wheeled devices that carry people and goods to their desired destination. And it is noisy. My senses are so sharpened that it is difficult to sort out sounds and images, my muddled brain having too much to do. I like it. This is Earth alive with sound and purpose, humanity stretching forth its wings, poised to soar above the clamor.

I wander without much thought, the sights sometimes quite disturbing. There are back alleys that are shrouded in gloom, the devil's lair where life is bought and sold without regard to the sanctity of spirit. There are the very poor who sleep on the sidewalk, a curled arm for a pillow, the breath of life so faint that it hovers in the air above their impoverished flesh, waiting for release to try again. And again.

I see families in rags, begging for food or coin; withered limbs, a child with cleft lip and palate pleading for pity, eyes locked on mine as I turn away.

I hear Jai calling me. I'm walking near the polo grounds, a vestige of the British Raj. There are many thin men hunkered down on the grass, a moving line of turbaned heads nodding as they attend to their work of cutting, the sickles rising and falling in synchronous rhythm as they slowly make their way forward, a silent line of duck-walking men who will never see a polo match but who will feed their families this day.

I hear Jai calling again and wrench my heart away from this scene and start walking back to the stone tower, which is a goodly distance away. *All right, all right, I'm coming.*

Jai bows and offers to fetch some breakfast.

"No, Jai. I'll be eating my usual meal at sunset. Please bring it then, with a knock on the door." I smile at the thought of this simple device that will pull me out of the dimensional worlds, a knock that I must answer. Jai then stations himself next to the door, sitting cross-legged on the cool marble floor, proof against evil spirits who may wish to disturb my captain and me.

The loud hum of the air conditioner blots out all other sounds in the darkened room.

As I sit with towel in hand, awaiting divine pleasure, I soon yelp as the position reasserts itself without any regard to comfort. The pain this day is red tinged and fretful with hand and arm contortions hard to suppress. I summon calmness and surrender to meet this upset, soon finding a pinpoint of light to follow in the black and red.

My hands relax and fall to my sides, the towel in my lap falling away, too. I'm dimly aware that there is no drool, nor will there be again. *Aha,* I think, *accommodation.* Time passes away to the timeless.

The knock on the door is quite insistent. Upon leaping up I tumble to the floor, my legs asleep and useless. *Well, shit,* I think, and call out, "A moment please, one moment."

I am sleeping on the sidewalk with one eye out for rats and vermin. My body is wracked with painful disease. I am alone and tortured with the desperation of the forgotten.

I see a vaporous beam snaking along the damp concrete and I watch as it arrives at my forehead. I am lifted, head and body still horizontal, and carried through the night air with the breeze of motion tingling my skin. I stretch out my arms and lift my head, smiling at the thought of Superman. With a whoosh of air and swirling cape, I land on my feet in front of a pure white gate brilliant with light.

"Oh, God," I say aloud as the dream fades into the nothingness from whence it came. I am still dressed, with boots on, my favored way to sleep. At least my clothes are clean now, thanks to Jai, who I discover is not outside my door, the hour too early at 5 a.m.

I brush my teeth and rework my braided hair. I gather up the goods I bought in Australia a lifetime ago, medicines and kitchenware, and ask the night clerk to call a taxi.

As the sky colors with violet and red, the taxi slowly proceeds along the dismal street where I recently lay asleep on the sidewalk. It is a horrible scene of destitution and poverty, even the closed shops broadcasting dreary enterprise. Then, in the glow of pearlescent light, the white gate appears on the right, a beacon in the darkest sea of suffering. I pay the taxi walla enough to keep him waiting.

When I begin to fear that the gate will never open—my repeated knocks echoing off into the damp air—a white- and blue-clad nun slides open a small window in the gate.

"Yes?"

"I've brought things for you, medicines and cutlery." I hold up the bag for her inspection. She says nothing. "I'm a medical doctor from America." At this, she nods and opens the gate to admit me.

"Thank you, kind sir," she says with a European accent. She is about 20 years old and quite beautiful in an unadorned way. "Mother Teresa is out of the country, but I accept these things in her name." She nods vigorously as I display the antibiotics and goods. There is light dancing around in the foyer where we are standing. I sense the presence of little ones, fairy-like beings, who are at play. I can't help but smile.

After five days in the chair, my head releases forward and I am done with it. I clap three times and open the black double doors, turning and bowing deeply to Jai, who had just come on duty. "I will be gone all day and will take a meal in the restaurant at sunset. You are..." (for a moment I can't find the proper word) "...released." He bows and backs away. I will never see him again.

Outside, the sun is streaming down in shafts of particulate light. I merge with the crowds of people on the sidewalk and let the flow take me where it will. Aha! A coconut vendor offers a green orb with a drinking straw of spiraled white and red. I gulp down the sweet milk until it's gone, carefully placing the coconut on a patch of grass near the sidewalk.

Vendors cry out in foreign tongues, hawking their goods from sidewalk stalls and carts. Incense fills the air as I wander among them, stopping now and then to touch exotic things.

After a time, I notice that there is a person following me at a distance, something that had been pushing at my awareness. He, a young man of 20 or so, dressed in white clothing, no turban or hat, stops when I stop, goes when I go, always 20 paces behind, never meeting my eye. *How odd*, I think, *how very odd*.

Stealing a glance over my left shoulder, I enter Victoria Gardens. Yes, he is still following me. I find a shaded bench under an arbor that looks out over a reflecting pool of still water. I can imagine Queen Victoria sitting on this very bench with the satisfaction of having tamed this wild city with a strong dose of English propriety.

A few seconds later, the young man appears and stops on the gravel path in front of me. He faces the reflecting pool without paying me any notice and starts throwing coins into the rippling water. I wonder at this unusual disregard for money by a person who can surely find better use for it. To my amazement, the young man starts twirling around in a spontaneous dance, arms uplifted in between throws of coins from his pocket: Around and around he goes, the water rippling anew with each toss. I am captivated by this display and begin to suspect that this is an important event and not just a random wonder. His dancing is somewhat awkward with him spinning in tight circles, arms outstretched. There is a neutral expression on his face, but his eyes are alight with intensity.

My mysterious friend concludes his dance and stands for a moment looking out over the water. He then turns and comes to the bench, sitting at my right side without meeting my gaze. We sit in silence for a time, both looking straight ahead. My astonishment at this ongoing sequence soon turns to expectant waiting: I know that this is a mystical event of some sort, and I summon patience. Perhaps it was a wait of a minute or two, but is, more accurately, a prolonged wait of 35 years. He slowly turns to me and lightly touches my right elbow with his right hand. Leaning close to my ear, he says in a clear voice, "I'm sorry." He quickly gets up and walks away, never to be seen again.

I am buoyant. I don't understand what has happened but know without a doubt I am forever changed as a result of his light touch on my right arm. Good Lord, what does it mean—*I'm sorry?*

Chapter Sixteen

London

And I, who neared the goal of all nature, felt my soul, at the climax of its yearning suddenly, as it ought, grow calm with rapture.
—Dante

I sit on the bench for a time, pondering this strange encounter. When nothing is forthcoming, I make my way back to the hotel and the stone tower's darkened room. No longer in a meditative phase, I consider packing up and leaving two days early. Instead, I decide to make a holiday of it and sit in a lounge chair in the courtyard watching myna birds fighting over food scraps.

That evening I take a meal of dal and rice in the dining room under the watchful eye of one of the two waiters I had seen almost a week before. The notion that time is passing and that I must get on with it—whatever that means—is thusly reinforced. That night I continue my habit of sleeping in my clothes with boots on. I am up and down all night pacing the darkened room with growing excitement. I pack up most of my things in the event that I must suddenly bolt for London, my next venue, even as the departure date is two days hence, but my restlessness is growing with each passing hour.

The next morning I awaken late. The sun is peeking through the drapes, making me feel like a young schoolboy who is in danger of missing the bus.

I know exactly what to do. After ablutions I hurry outside and make my way through the growing crowds on the busy streets. *Quickly now, make haste,* my mind tells my feet. I scurry along, intent on business, ignoring all distractions, until I reach Victoria Gardens and find the exact same spot on the bench where I sat the day before. And I wait, looking out over the calm water, its surface still and undisturbed. And I wait.

I notice the scent of jasmine drifting on the torpid air, and as I turn my head to seek out its source, the fingers on my left hand begin to move spontaneously in a rapid sequence, each independent of the others, much like playing a tune on a piano, a musical skill that I had not acquired. My shock at this surprising thing is greatly moderated by the blissful feeling that comes with the finger movements. My left thumb also is moving rapidly, a cadence somehow connected to the four fingers in a meaningful way. Oh yes, this is exactly right, I think, and I lift my hand into the air above my left knee and watch the whirring movement, my fingers now a blur of motion, impossible to match with voluntary intent. Soon my entire arm is involved, rising up and down, here and there, with the breath of bliss enveloping my senses. *This is magnificent,* I think. I am alive with purpose. The eye of my mind is finally open, but what a surprising thing it is to have a part of my physical form respond to commands and input that come from somewhere beyond my conscious intent.

Any alarm that came forth is almost instantly countered by two things: bliss, the flowing feeling of incredible well-being that floats my mind in a sea of ecstasy, and the immediate recognition that my finger motions are very much like those of Meher Baba that I had seen on film. Aha!

I sit on the bench for some time, perhaps for hours, watching and experiencing the complex faculty that has been opened in my consciousness. The muscles in my left forearm eventually tire and I cautiously will my fingers to stop. They do. Is this a one-time thing or would they begin the dance again? I mentally relax the stop order and, yes, they resume, perhaps more furiously than before. *This is me at work. This...is...me...at...work*, I intone with my fingers in the air.

I keep my hand down at my side as I return to the streets once again, my fingers assuming new tempos as we walk along. I say *we* because I am an entire orchestra and not just one player. I feel connected in ways that are well beyond the province of ego mind. *I have taken my place at the oaken table of my dream long ago.* Yes, I am wearing wrinkled khakis instead of a long purple robe dancing with light, my beard brown and not yet white, but it is so, nonetheless.

Sleep is out of the question. I sit in a chair throughout the night attentive to...what? I'm not certain. The activity of my left hand is purposeful and even powerful, but I have absolutely no insight into what I'm actually doing. It is like playing the piano blindfolded without hearing the notes struck, but I know without a doubt that the music is beautiful. I can almost hear it.

The dawn brings with it *possibilities*. The feeling of expectation becomes a powerful engine that has me leaping down the stone steps to the courtyard and thence to the streets. I am intent on returning to the magical bench of yesterday—out of my way, out of my way! As I'm dodging people and obstacles in my path, I note that the motion of my fingers on the left hand has slowed to a stop—as do I. I look at my left hand in puzzlement, only to feel the fingers of my right hand slowly begin the same dance. A surge of bliss encapsulates my heart and spreads throughout my body as the right hand begins adding a bassline to the dimensional music. It is slower, more labored, seemingly requiring more effort as I allow this new wonder to unfold.

"Okay, okay," I say aloud, and start slowly proceeding again. Walking now takes thought because much of my mind is centered on the activity of my right hand. There is much more power herein, the connection to conscious thought more direct; *my fingers and mind become entwined in a union of metaphysical completeness.*

I take care not to stumble as I make my way to Victoria Gardens and the magical bench. Once there, I sit and allow various dimensions to find increasing resonance within my physical form.

After the sun has made a slow journey to its zenith, I notice the fingers of my left hand begin to dance once again, entirely separate from the motions of the right, yet synchronous and pleasing as both coordinate in fast-paced rhythms of infinite complexity. I am astonished at this completely unexpected occurrence, this visible manifestation of ordered change in non-visible dimensions, a blending of the seen and unseen that gives depth and breadth to my singular existence on earth. I am fully here at last, although the *Who am I?* part of the question remains unanswered.

So, what is this hand business? I had little idea at the time, but pressing questions are always answered eventually. Years later, I would discover a name for these movements: *mudras*, which are purposeful movements of the human form that are connected to higher dimensions. They are latent in every human being on Earth, but are only activated in some—a precious gift of personal attainment as well as a curse of sorts. Unlike superpowers or magic, mudras work only in the universal sense and never for personal gain.

From that remarkable day in Victoria Gardens to the present, the mudras have been a constant in my life, almost continuous, even in dream sequences. I soon learn to accomplish tasks leaving one hand free for this dimensional work. I also learn to conceal this unusual behavior from casual observation by any but my closest family and associates.

Going forward, as my consciousness expanded, other mudras would develop, most notably the toes, tongue, and internal organs to some degree. Human anatomy is much more complicated than is usually thought.

The 10-passenger plane is cramped and noisy as we fly low over the countryside on the way to Pune. At one point during the flight, I sense that we are directly over the Om point, the foremost of all primary spots in the creation—square one, if you like, of all that is. It is an engrossing feeling of mystical treasure, of comfort and power mixed with an oldness that is beyond ancient. The actual geography is unremarkable: rolling hills with scattered trees. There is no habitation that I can see.

My eight fingers and two thumbs are a blur of motion as we pass over it, giving rise to a question from my elderly seatmate, an Englishwoman.

"Are you practicing piano?" she asks.

"Why, yes I am," I say, grinning. She nods and we resume our noisy silence until the plane touches down in Pune, whereupon she wishes me good luck. I wish her the same and throw in a little dimensional well-wishing, too. I quickly proceed to the taxi stand for the final leg to Ahmednagar.

As I am lugging my prayer rug out of the rickshaw at the trust compound in Ahmednagar, it strikes me that it is time to give it away. Pat Sumner had mentioned in passing that it was Eruch's birthday, so I seek him out. As I present the rug to him without explanation, he nods but says nothing. He is not pleased at all.

On later visits, I would find the rug on the floor of Mandali Hall and even would have occasion to sit upon it, listening to Eruch's stories of life with Meher Baba.

It wouldn't occur to me until several years later that the young man who danced for me in Calcutta was indeed the perfect master that I had sought.

Sometimes, particularly during or just after an advent of the Ancient One, perfect masters remain undercover, hidden in the folds of general humanity, known as such to only a few of their closest people.

As a *pilgrim* on Earth arrives at the great abyss between the sixth and seventh planes of consciousness, the physical touch of a perfected soul is necessary to make the leap.

So it was that my young friend transmitted the *power* and *love* that combined is the engine of transport from the unreal to the real. If I had recognized him at the time, I would have given him the damn rug.

John Connor, Bhau's secretary, finds me just as I'm about to depart. "Bhau has a sore hip and would like you to attend to him."

To say that I am surprised understates the case. I hadn't advertised that I was a doctor, and in view of our difficult encounter before, the request is entirely unexpected. John leads me to his room but warns that I am not to touch Bhau or talk to him directly.

As I stand at the foot of Bhau's bed where he reclines fully dressed, John repeats, "Bhau has a sore right hip. What should he do?"

"Does it hurt him to walk?" I ask John.

"Yes, it does," John replies as Bhau remains silent.

"Well, I recommend acetylsalicylic acid 325 milligrams twice daily." Bhau nods and motions for me to leave.

Aspirin.

Eventually I make my way to the airport in Bombay, the details of travel almost beyond my capabilities—I am floating in a cloud of dimensional mist of pink and violet. *Don't bother me, please, anyone.*

"You're a day early," the British Airways lady advises. "We can get you on a flight at 5 a.m. if you like."

Although I had quit smoking cigarettes a few months before, I buy a pack and sit up all night smoking them one after the other.

After not sleeping for several days, I am truly exhausted as I sit in the roomy back seat of a black London taxicab. As we approach Hyde Park, I lean forward and tap the glass. "Please take me to lodging where I will be comfortable."

"'Tisn't allowed, sir. You must declare a destination," he says, looking at me in the rearview mirror with eyebrows raised.

"Look, I'm so tired that I can't think properly."

We drive on for a while before he replies, "I have a cousin who runs a B&B on Earl's Court in Kensington..." I wave him on.

At 5 a.m., the driver's repeated knocks on the door bring no response. He turns to walk back to the cab when the door finally is opened by a matronly woman with sleep-tousled hair.

"Oh yes, Clyde," she says.

I don't hear the rest of their conversation, but I soon have a room upstairs at a good price. The stout woman explains that the W.C. is down the hall to the left, and breakfast will be served at half past 6. "Yes ma'am," I respond.

"Right, then," says Mrs. Smythe as I pay a week in advance.

The room is quite small, with a narrow bed, a dresser with a mirror above it, a small desk and chair, and a glorious window with a view of similar brick row houses across the way, plus some trees, too. I open the window to admit a cool breeze and am asleep before my head hits the pillow.

The morning crisp with promise, I sit in the chair facing the window. I know without a doubt that I've arrived at the very last stepping-stone to the infinite. I have not a care in the world and feel only love in my heart for all that is, all that was, and all that will be. I pause a moment to embrace this feeling, this perfect feeling of absolute satisfaction. God is in his heaven and I will soon join him there. What happens thereafter, I care not. My fingers and hands orchestrate the great hall where the host awaits, sounds and feelings soon quieting as the Maestro appears to thunderous applause. Then, silence. The white baton flashes once, twice, then...

My head falls to my knees, my arms dangle to the floor, my fingers and hands go silent and still. I am pluripotential, a nothing that waits for something to stir. My mind witnesses and records impressions, fleeting and wispy, of no consequence whatsoever. I matter not, a mere pinpoint in the vastness of Self that is the circular mind of God. I see my pinpoint of denseness flash into explosive light that sings a single note of awareness that is itself a circle, one divided into eight arcs.

I disappear and become the vastness that is nothing—with no recording mind at all. And yet, I hear birds chirping and feel a breath of air. WHO IS THIS? *A question that bypasses my mind to become itself the infinite answer that circles the question forever...*

IT IS I.

Time must surely be passing as I remain in place before the glorious window. It is time, after all, that pushes awareness into a circle. *I exist; therefore, time is passing*—a theorem of some delight. Time stops. Time begins. Time...

Well, let's lift up then. My head raises.

I'm not alone. My volition is coming from somewhere else, an infinite part that seems to know everything there is to know. This part thinks like my captain thinks, and is what lifts my head, but it keeps my eyes closed. We stand. We waltz three steps. I have no idea where I am or when. Then I record a bundle of sensation that is hugely surprising: my head is upside down and my feet are swinging up and over. I land on the softness of the bed, my feet hitting the wall—a somersault! My brain starts working hard to sort out this thing done in the dark. My eyes don't open, but I struggle upright, swinging limbs and watching thoughts as they come and go. Yes, I'm standing once again, the *where* and *when* still an open question.

The infinite part of my system whips me upward again, ass over teakettle, and flops me on the bed, my feet *thunking* on the wall a little harder than before: number two. Two somersaults now. My mind registers this phenomenon and I realize that I'm in room 204, the *where* of the question now answered. And it is funny, this *thunking* the wall with scuffed-up boots. Lord knows who is on the other side of the wall. Why am I doing this? Of course, it is not I doing this, I remind myself. Standing again, this time knowing the game, I tense up a bit, waiting. Nothing happens, so I relax. Aha! There it is again, *thunk* one foot, *thunk* the next.

This time, I know we're done with the game of *where*, and with the surprising gymnastics of human body on bed that aroused me from slumber. Alright already, I'm almost *awake*.

I stand and turn, waltzing in darkness across the room. My eyes then pop open, and who do I see? Myself, reversed in the mirror: brown eyes, brown hair, brown beard, mouth moving. "Baba," I say, with the index finger of my right hand pointing at the image in the mirror. "Baba." And just to make certain, a third time, "Baba." I don't like it, this *who* business. I shun this *Baba* thought that is so insistent. There is a *we* that remains unexplained, inviting further investigation.

I turn from the mirror. Is it me that is really doing this? I think not. How do I feel? I feel marvelous, filled with wonder and bliss. There is a raspberry flavor on my tongue and jasmine in the air. I'm alive with expectation; I am great to behold. I am perfect.

My fingers are moving again as I stand in the center of the room. *I* walk one step at a time to the door and fumble at the latch. So it is that *I* plod down the hall in present time and exact tempo to the W.C. *We* enter and listen to the sounds of life that come through the floor and walls.

The window opens to our touch, admitting cool air. A twist of knobs, and water pounds into the tub full force. Undressing requires great attention to unbutton and unbuckle. The lingam rises and begs for worship, but no, it is bathing that settles and cleans. The infinite parts of fingers and mind find place within time and flesh. We coordinate and vibrate with purpose.

There is an orbiting essence of female that settles in as well. This receptive part becomes entranced with jasmine and weaves surrender into the matrix of self. This part loves the smell of soapy suds and winks at me with an internal smile; such love she has.

Wet hair dances on my cold neck. I place the houndstooth cap atop my head and straighten my red knit tie, tucking it under the blue woolen sweater.

The outside air is pungent with English smells as we walk with increasing skill and ease. Everything is a surprise, because it is not I, but we, and I'm along for the ride. We enter a café and order eggs and sausage—a rare thing, breakfast. I listen to London talk amongst the blue-collars who work for a living—*mate* this, *bloody* that, *right then*, with a slap on the back, *mate*. Who's this then, sitting among us? Looks a yank, an odd one at that; I hear their mind's question float over to me—I say aloud, "Yes, it's an odd yank, indeed," although the question wasn't actually spoken.

Pushing my eggs around on the plate, I reflect on how odd this yank truly is: an encyclopedia salesman turned ear surgeon who took his Harley for a ride to other dimensions and now sits in a London café reading the minds of mates across the way. These thoughts wobble my thinking into a vertiginous spin. I slap some cash on the table and totter outside, acute indigestion my new friend of the moment.

I wait on the station platform, looking down the shiny rails. Far in the distance, I hear the mournful whistle, a lingering echo overridden by a rumble and chug. She'll be coming 'round the mountain when she comes...

Church bells awaken me from a brief slumber the next bright morning, the deep European tones ecclesiastical, but also cheerful. Various odd jerks of my limbs remind me that I have a new operating system that isn't quite in sync. Nonetheless, I bound out of bed and wash up.

I wonder, wonder who, who wrote the book of love, who wrote the book of love...Who? My hands are a blur of motion. I see them in the mirror.

I seem to be walking quite normally with the glaring exception of absence of volition; it is, therefore, a carefree walk. The sky is brightly blue with various shades of pink and violet intensely intermingled. Discarded leaves of autumn scurry, everywhere bending to the will of a cool breeze at play. Kensington Road is quite busy with traffic, as is the sidewalk where I amble in partnership with leaf and breeze, passersby each broadcasting a story even as they try to hide their minds from view.

Who wrote the book of love, who wrote...

Of a sudden, I turn left from the sidewalk and pound across the artery of busy cars on Kensington Road. *Good Lord,* I think, not having looked to left or right. I'm just proceeding across it with a hope and a... No, no, prayer is not necessary. It will be fine—and it is. *Whew!* Now I stand on the other side of the whizzing thoroughfare, but it still isn't the perfect destination, it appears. So, back again I heel and toe, eyes straight ahead, ears alert for honk and screech, but I've found the moving interstice of perfect safe passage. *Whew,* indeed.

I stand on the sidewalk once again, hands on hips, noting the impossibility of what I've just done, the congested lanes of colorful cars almost on top of one another in the snaky lines of a conga dance.

Of a sudden, I bound across Kensington Road, *again,* in the spirit of *you ain't seen nothin' yet.*

And so it goes, back and forth, forth and back, no horns, no screeches, no paddy wagon, no nuthin.' I could do this all day— and it seems that I have. We have an operating system that takes *everything* into account. There is no chance for misstep, no chance for error, no unknowns at all. I am perfect and always have been. I look down at my toes, my boots, and see that I'm ready to dance to a dozen tunes at a time, jiggity-jig.

After a dozen trips across Kensington Road, it's done, and I'm stationed again on the original sidewalk in one piece. With a vigorous shake of burbled head, I quit this game and enter Hyde Park.

People wander on paths, as do I—here and there, I notice a few flowers in tended beds along the way that have yet to bend to winter's knee. All this damn walking prompts a rest on a bench near a fountain where trickles of water-music fill the silence, the sun's rays dancing between leaf and bough.

I'm alone, or so it seems; but never really alone again.

I begin tapping a single finger on my knee, with a word coming in with each tap:

You-*tap*-are-*tap*-my-*tap*-greatest-*tap*-lover.

Water-music soothes my mind as I process this unexpected, unlikely news from...where? My beyond self.

You-*tap*-are-*tap*-the-*tap*-greatest-*tap*-American. What? I barely consider myself American at all.

You-will-usher-in-the-new-age.

Well, that's something, at least.

I-will-always-be-with-you.

Yes, this I know.

There is more of this electrifying discourse. It is the only such experience that I will ever have with my captain from Beyond, the Maestro, before a seamless bonding makes such things impossible.

I sit on the bench for a time, my mind tossing around the input until it settles into place for later review. I feel like heaven has opened its arms to enfold me even as I sit on a bench in Hyde Park, London. I am flooded with gratitude and wonder beyond imagining. All this, all this.

Soon my feet instruct me to walk over to a nearby tree, and I oblige. I kneel at its woody roots and gush out sobs that erupt from an unsuspected reservoir of human grief. On and on it goes, wrenching sobs as my hands latch on to a splayed tree root, my anchor to the Earth. My tears are diamonds that glisten on fallen leaves. I reach down and scatter these leaves until the diamonds are hidden again and enfolded into autumnal earth.

Sitting back on my heels, alive and free, it is done. I know who I am: I am the essence of all that is, that which eyes cannot see nor mind decipher. I am beyond mind with eternal existence flowing through my veins. I am flesh and bone powered by love and purpose—and I have no name. If you must call me something, let it be *Ichen.*

Oh Lord, there is a pressing urgency; I must go now. I must leave London, but first there is a task. I know exactly what to do.

I trot to Embassy Row before slowing to a speedy walk. There it is—Chile. I stand for a moment on a transported slice of orchard near the Chilean coast. I do work and move on. Namibia, a slice of barren veld. I work and move on. New Zealand, a rocky cliff above the pounding sea. Then I briskly walk on to Poland. I love this one, a stall in a farmer's market. I see Lech Walesa working on a motorbike. I move on...

It takes most of the day. I feel the chill of evening as I finally quit the bench and water-music and slowly walk back to Mrs. Smythe's B&B.

Chapter Seventeen

New York City

God provides thread for the work begun.
—James Howell

As I had hoped, the London American Express office does have an envelope for me, the last payment from my medical practice that I convert to Traveler's Checks.

"Can I get an earlier flight to New York?" I ask the agent.

"Let's see." She scans for availability. "If you can get to Heathrow in an hour, it'll work, sir, aisle seat."

The flight attendants are somewhat concerned when I decline all food and drink but water. Unlike my fellow passengers, I stay awake all night, furiously working mudras that I conceal under the fold-down tray. I stare at the glass of water on the tray, watching the plane's motion jiggle it about before finally draining the glass in one gulp as the plane begins its descent.

What now? The only emotion that surfaces is urgency, the most pressing thought is that I'm running out of time. Where to stay? I've never been to New York and have no idea about hotels. My head is swimming with *almost thoughts* that have little relevance to travel concerns. What little is left of my thinking brain begins to worry. At this juncture a word pops up—*Biltmore*—and I relax: I have a destination.

Since I had given away all my camping gear and was no longer burdened by the rug, all I owned in the world was contained in a backpack and leather suitcase that was easy to lug around. I watch for them on the turning carousel, getting dizzy in the process.

The lady at the hotel desk in the baggage area has news for me. "The Biltmore was torn down two years ago."

"Well, what do you recommend?" I ask her.

"The Beverly Hotel has a vacancy."

"Good enough."

So, Biltmore gets me to the Beverly. I am learning how things work: Spirit may direct, but not necessarily the way an oracle would. I will have to weave in Earthly context.

The Beverly in Manhattan is a dreary affair, a brownstone façade with a small neon sign and no doorman. I don't care a whit; *Let's get to it.*

I open the drapes of the small, fuzzy room. The window overlooks other dirty windows on the building across the way. I close the drapes and set the chair in the middle of the room and enter the mystical folds of the colossal dream. This is my work, my mission on earth: *to rework the dream of Isa.*

Several days have passed with me in the chair at the Beverly, and I'm no closer to a solution. I have repeatedly made arduous visits to the Om point, which has a secondary aspect in New York City. Nonetheless, I can't quite get it. I thought it would be easy, but it isn't at all. Each time I retrain original vectors, Universal Sanskaras, something goes awry. Moreover, I'm starting to lose my physicality, a worrisome deterioration that continues day by day in spite of my best efforts to reverse it. My mind is a muddle, barely aware of my surroundings, as dreary as they may be. I haven't eaten much; fruit and water that came with the room is the extent of it.

I'm working on the very frontier of the creation, where Isa's dream pushes 1 into 3 and then into 2. Because it is always the beginning and always the end, the original impulse, the sound of Om, the light of Isa is everywhere and *every when*—it's not distant in time or space; it is here in the Beverly Hotel, and I'm interfacing with it as a fully conscious human being with something to do. The problem is really an urgent one. At the time I didn't fully realize how urgent. The causal energy flowing through my system is so powerfully charged that it starts burning up my neural circuits and internal organs. I have about three days before my physical body would be irreversibly damaged. After six days, death of the body would return me to Universality from whence I came.

Although I didn't know these awful details at the time, I could tell that my situation was dire indeed.

The mind of God is circular while the human mind is linear; cause and effect is linear and is logical while the mind of Isa is circular, allowing such conundrums as the chicken and egg to confound human intellect. The dream, therefore, is a mishmash of linear and circular motives that defies easy dissection. It requires special tools, mudras, as it were, and the timing must be exact—a small window of opportunity.

The circle of past, present, and future spews forth dream images that acquire rationality and form to appear in the visible world. The actual process of manifestation is much like an assembly line where a basic product becomes fully completed in several steps. The steps in this case are processes that occur in higher dimensions, of which there are seven, each more rational than the previous one, each work station a circular world in itself.

My task is to correct minute irrationality in the system that allows final products to be misshapen. Because I stand at the interface of linear and circular thought, mudras, which are interdimensional moderators of energetic flow, can alter systems that are in place. I am not alone in this work. There are five other guardians on Earth that stand at the interface, as did my captain while he was earthbound. *Moreover, my task is to find personal compatibility within the system, a place within it that sustains my physicality while I work in nonphysical dimensions.*

Thus far, I have failed—I have not found a workable solution, nor have I found a place of succor to prevent personal destruction as I wield these energies. Time is running out, even though time is circular and never runs out. Time is infused in the water of my body, and because my current work is outside of time, it is a matter of a few days before the cells in my body cease to function in the visible world and I revert to Reality from whence the dream comes. There is a certain allure to this prospect that I must fight; this I know.

The chair in the center of the room is like a rock on the beach, the sands of time flowing all around it. After a while, I stand and leave the rock to re-enter time—to rest and allow my body to repair some of the cellular damage. I'm not certain what day it is but can tell that a lot of time has passed. I walk down the carpeted hall to the ice machine and fill a small bucket with chunks of frozen water. Water holds time within its molecules, hydrogen being the first element in the visible world. Although it exists elsewhere in small quantities, time rests most comfortably in water.

I carry the bucket back to room 1506, where a Do Not Disturb sign hangs on the door, and plunge my right hand into the ice. Soon the intense pain has my mind functioning more normally. After a brief rest, I quit the room and take the coffin-like elevator to the lobby, where its glass doors exit to the world beyond.

The cold wind of Manhattan blows the leaves of my existence to and fro; I am cold in a distant way. I walk the sidewalks of late morning, people greeting me now and then. They smile and I flash a grin and whip my fingers around their auras. I love this place, New York.

A sandwich and beer? A tavern appears and I enter with this in mind. All I have in my wallet are hundred-dollar bills. I proffer one to the bartender.

"Sorry, can't change it," he says.

"What should I do?"

"There's a bank next block," he says.

If he only knew how hard it is to move, he might have fetched it himself. So be it.

I present a bill to the teller, who obliges me with assorted lesser bills. She smiles and wishes me a good day.

I remember that it is the bartender who sent me here, so I return to his polished and mirrored palace. This time I notice a room to the left that has musical instruments hanging on the wall, a saxophone, trumpet, and guitar on display, a piano up on stage. A jazz club by night, the bartender explains as I eat and drink with consummate pleasure. "Come back tonight," he suggests. Inwardly, I laugh at the thought, so far removed am I from such things. So far.

Back in 1506 I find my rock and sit, watching the swirls of past and future as I subsist entirely in the present, furiously working

through the miasma of causation. I change tactics and stop trying to find errors of translation as vectors work through the seven
steps. Instead, I try to find a place to stand, an internal configura-
tion that permits time to function in my cellular makeup even as I
continue to consciously exist in the six higher worlds where time is
increasingly translucent. No small task.

All the water is gone, as are the oranges. The closed drapes
are darker than before, which I take to mean that night has snuck
in. Am I done? Is it done? I can't really tell, but I'm exhausted. I
pry myself up and dip toes into the vortices of swirling time. Ah,
it works. I stand and wobble to the window, throwing drapes aside.
Yes, it is dark. My wristwatch is somewhere or other, and, upon
finding it, 9 p.m., it says. There is no music in my mind and hasn't
been for a long while—I want music more than food or beer, the
tavern a place for all three.

Outside, it is cold, with steam issuing from subterranean blow-
holes, a hissing sound. I walk on metal grates in the sidewalk, which
ground my feet far better than concrete. It takes some gymnastic
skill to heel and toe the metal grates, my mind thusly occupied
with each step. Oddly, many passersby say hello and smile, perhaps
a "How ya doing?" thrown in. "Fine, fine," I say, with gratitude that
bounces back and forth between us before we go our separate ways.
I recognize some of these people, my extended family as it were,
brief encounters that hold great worth, it seems.

Aha, the tavern at last. I leave the metal grate and enter. All
ideas about food and drink vanish in the blink of an eye, for my
eyes duly record that the jazz room on the left is no longer there.
The rest of the polished and mirrored barroom is just as it was. The
bartender is at work with the briefest glance my way, no recognition forthcoming, no smile. I have no smile for him either, horror
my main emotion at this travesty of translation. I know this *alteration*

is unfavorable because it makes my head spin with regret and despair. *I have failed*; this I know.

Back in room 1506, the rock seems to be gone, although the chair remains. I'm stuck in a *somewhere* with disastrous results. I sense that the entire constellation of the present is riddled with undesirable non sequiturs, not just this one.

I flop on the bed and fall into a sleep that is punctuated by surreal images of demons floating just out of reach—not that I would have wanted to capture one in any event. At least they are unable to reach me. So far, they can't.

Fully awake now, I realize that the partner of my failure is personal death. Joe Black is the one smiling at me now as he patiently awaits his time. My heart races with the thought of this, the final dance, and my mind calls out for surcease. Just as a young soldier dying on a distant battlefield cries out for his mother, I want to go home.

Of course, I have no home.

My folks are glad to hear from me after many months of silence. I had sent them occasional telegrams along the way, but they have no idea what I'm up to.

"Where are you?" Dad asks.

I'm-in-New-York." I reply, my cadenced speech difficult to manage and no doubt alarming to them.

"What's wrong, Dick?"

"Oh-I'm-just-tired-Mother." We both realize that I never call her mother. Mom it is, *Mom.*

I shake my head, which causes lavender vapor to be disturbed in the air around me as I stand with phone to ear. I try harder to normalize. I stop my mudras.

"Anyway," I say, with more volume, "I'd like to visit you in Northampton for a few days if it's okay."

"Ah, when?" Dad asks.

"Well, dear Father-how-about-now?" There is silence on the phone as intense parental calculation takes place in heavy time. My hands are moving again.

"I'll take a shuttle from Logan," I say. Having visited them once before, I can probably get there on my own.

"No, I'll pick you up. Call when you get in," Dad says.

Grateful dead or dying, I think. Home. Joe Black wants to come along on this visit, too, but I plead with him to wait, to stay behind.

Blue chambray shirt, red knit tie, blue sweater, khakis, scuffed boots—check. Suitcase—check. Pay the bill—check. Taxi with Middle Eastern driver—check. LaGuardia and commuter plane nausea—check. *Oh, God deliver me. Where is Baba in all this?*

It is only later that I put it together. The Ancient One is the *preserver* of the creation, and my dimensional work involved *causation*, a new system to replace the old one, which was *dissolved.* Hence, I was on my own, so to speak, my Baba center shut down.

I had never ridden in an American Motors Pacer before, a ridiculous car that Dad loves. Our few attempts at conversation curdle like sour milk on a hot sidewalk. He's blinking furiously, gripping the steering wheel with white knuckles, as I grip the armrest with my right and blur the fingers on the left. Who cares at this point?

The Pacer is filled with furious vectors, all calling out for attention. There is nothing on my stomach to expel, but the nausea comes in waves of portent.

I fall getting out of the damn car. The desperation has me sweating as I right myself to greet Mother-Mom on the steps. I had forgotten that her hair is still red; it's only later that it goes white. The steps are concrete, the house red brick with a steeply pitched roof; it snows here.

There are tears as we embrace, but they are mine, not hers. I read her thoughts and agree: I'm a mess, a shocking mess. The causative energy running through my veins has damaged my cellular workings to the degree that organs are starting to shut down— just as if I were drinking again, which gives me an idea.

"Okay, okay, I know," I say to her. Inside the foyer, I turn to Dad. "Please buy me a fifth of bourbon, a fifth of scotch, and a fifth of vodka." So strong is my presence that he just nods and leaves for the package store.

I take Mom by the hand and we go sit in the living room. "What-dear-Mother-do-you-most-regret-in-your-life?" She immediately responds, gushing forth an event that has caused her much grief. I wipe it out, and as she weeps, I wander off to take a hot shower, leaving her asleep on the couch.

Refreshed and more centered, I help Dad carry in the bottles of spirits and put them in a cabinet under the sink. I will not drink any of it, but the idea is there—an alcoholic relapse, an easier thing for them to live with than the truth, which can never be told, at least in its fullness, ever.

For lunch, Dad suggests a nearby café, not that I can eat, but a cup of tea perhaps. As we are walking, we pass a secondhand furniture/junk shop featuring a sign out front that reads *Doorbulbs and Lightknobs*. I stop to work this out. Does it make sense? My gut makes it clear, but I ask Dad anyway.

"What does that sign read?" He steps back and peers at the sign.

"Doorbulbs and Lightknobs," he declares defensively. "What of it?"

Another anomaly, there is little question. This time I am lifted off the earth and back into the miasma where in fact I locate the anomalous vectors. I'm crushed. There is no obvious repair other than starting over once again.

We never make it to the café, our shared upset far too great.

I'm not afraid of dying, having already experienced its prelude. I'm very much afraid of failing, though, particularly with distortions still in place: the current dream is a nightmare that casts a pall over the House where I reside.

The utter humiliation of asking my aging parents to help me undress becomes the lingering memory of that awful time. The cold shower helps a great deal and I retire to the upper room and an army cot to sleep the afternoon and night away.

At 2 a.m. I arise and dress, including my red knit tie. I go through the house making subtle changes, moving a pencil from the kitchen to the den. I take down a blue vase from the mantle and place it on the coffee table. I switch a few books in the book-case and take Tennessee out of a child's puzzle of the states, placing it facedown nearby. I tread softly up the stairs to the upper room to rest on the cot until dawn.

The smell of brewing coffee noxious, I creep down the stairs, suitcase in hand. All of us fully dressed, we sit at the kitchen table.

Dad is furious. "I don't know what is going on with you, but we can't take it anymore." He pauses, turning slightly away to look at Mom. "We want you to leave...now." Even though I know this was coming, a lump in my throat keeps me from speaking.

Mom then says with a tremulous voice, "Put everything back the way it was." I nod, the work already done. I will oblige her.

I have not found succor and am dying cell by cell. Dad's plea, the only reasonable one, pushes me out the door where my failure greets me. I take one step forward... I take one step forward...

As the plane descends at LaGuardia, I see the complex footprint of the city, gray concrete stretching up to overcast sky. I know how to do it this time. I have met failure and not blinked; my sight now seems open. Why? I don't know. I don't see Joe Black anywhere.

I check in at the Waldorf Astoria, the roaring '20s gilt and ornate moldings somehow satisfying. There are fresh flowers in the foyer, well-dressed people who say hello, and perfume fragrances that matrons leave in their wake—gifts to me with my immediate thanks given.

This time the room is spacious and clear, a distant era's luxury still comforting; heavy floral drapes and antique plumbing weaving a timeless spell. Room 808, Gabriel's lair.

There is little time left—there are holes in my aura and vacuous spaces between organ cells that scream for attention. I sit, pulling my mind away from my body's insistent cries. I re-enter the pluripotential miasma and swim upstream through the turbid waters of time to the *source*, the bright light of 1-2-3 from whence all sound emanates. The sound descends like a waterfall into seven pools, each spilling into the next lower one. Yes, I have been here before. I look at this scene with my right eye this time, whereupon the pools present as seven worlds, each connected in sequence by complex threads of time and light, flowing, flowing, one to the next. And then I see it, a slight incongruity in the sixth world that enlarges in the fifth, increasing with each descending level until minute divergence from perfection disturbs the dream itself. As does the Earth: each world slowly spins to form a Universal Chakra. As this system comes into focus, I intuit the solution: a system of energetic shields around each world that function as global barriers with small gates that prevent direct flow of imperfect vectors through the system, each gate a temporal *opening* attended to by archangels or angels at each level.

Each open gate in the barrier has a defined locus that orbits at a different velocity in each world. The chance of all gates lining up at once to allow mischievous vectors to course through the entire system and then manifest in the visible world, *infinitesimal*, but extant. The possibility of imperfection is thusly preserved, and rightly so.

Immediately the deterioration of my physicality is slowed, but not entirely stopped. As I look down at my booted feet, I find no stable place to stand. I sense Gabriel at my right elbow but can't see him. I sense an unseen angel at my left elbow as the two of them support me above the latticework of existence—my feet dangling in the void. In a burst of sudden insight, I perceive the ultimate solution. *The unstable system of seven dimensions and seven worlds must be supplanted by a system of eight. The awakening of the dormant eighth dimension is the solution that allows my feet to find purchase and for my physicality to be maintained—albeit with effort.*

What I hear now is a different song, one based on Octave, but admitting a lesser chord of six. Gabriel sings the six-note song, as the six of us, the five guardians and I, raise our voices in an eight-note melody that fills the universe with *complexity and bliss.* It is a new sound that enters the oceans of Earth. The porpoises and whales show their delight. As Gabriel's song is drifting away and my right elbow is released, I feel the angel on my left depart as well. I ask, "Who are you?" as he takes his leave.

"Gamiel," he replies. I hastily write this down on hotel stationery. "Is this right?" I ask, holding up the scribbled word. "It is," he says, before he too is gone. I had not heard of Gamiel but later discover that he is the angelic counterpart of Gabriel, the chief archangel.

I'm back in room 808. The feeling that I have is the exact feeling that I experienced in Shaw's Cove when I learned of my mission on Earth. The wonderful difference is that I have accomplished this very mission—and am still here, mostly in one piece.

The eighth dimension, reflected in the eighth human chakra, is a composite of the other seven levels in a circular redundancy that keeps Isa's dream alive and well guarded from the unintended consequences of low-probability events, or *maya*. This is the net result of my work in New York.

I tip over the chair in my haste to get a bucket of ice. I prop open the door and careen down the hall to no avail—no ice machine. Back to the room, I call room service and tick off the moments with jabs to my palm with a pocket knife. The liveried porter, a young man, is family. We exchange pleasantries while he rights the chair and opens the drapes. I ask him for a vase of flowers, iris if possible.

I plunge my left hand into the silver bucket until the searing pain is unbearable. Then the right. I feel circuits in my brain burning up faster than I can ice them. I lurch into the quaint bathroom and look into the mirror, and all I see is the *ninth visage*: reality reflected in the house of mirrors. I gasp at the vertiginous ecstasy that comes slithering up my spine. I recoil in horror and plunge my hand into the bucket again and again. I fight the allure of reunion, but it isn't nearly enough.

The Maestro mounts the stage, the orchestra silent and waiting, the performance now over and done. As his baton lifts, the musicians stand and bow before leaving the stage. Again the white baton commands, as the heavy blue curtain slowly comes down. As I watch this scene unfold, the Maestro turns to me, his baton raised high as is his other hand. Slowly, slowly, his baton and left hand drift down, his shrouded eyes locked on mine. I bow to my waist then fall to my knees as the veil descends over my open eyes. I stand and bow once again. There is no applause as I exit stage right, my hands extended in front of me. I can't see any more—I can't see any when.

There is a knock on the door. The young porter bears a large vase of cut flowers, iris among them. He smiles.

By 2 a.m. I'm feeling well enough that the idea of company is appealing. New York City never sleeps, it seems, so I wander the streets saying hello to people and petting leashed dogs. I hum a tune as the brisk night air fills my lungs with Earth time. I see a well-dressed couple enter an all-night café, her jewels sparkling in the street-light glow. The gentleman is dressed in tails and a top hat, the scene reminiscent of a 1930s movie.

There is no guard at the door, and I simply walk in. The yellow light inside illuminates a lively scene of waitresses shouting orders to several short-order cooks and diners leaning across tables, their intimate thoughts and words drifting to and fro in the smoky air. I snatch some of these precious thoughts and drink them in as soulful nourishment, me standing near the door. A waitress points to an empty table where a vase with a single rose beckons. I gratefully sit and smell the floral essence, the seat across the table empty... or is it? Laughter pulses the room's yellow light and I see golden threads of timeless *love* dance and weave the *perfect stories of shared earthly life; imperfection, the unlovely stepchild, waiting in the wings.*

I order a cup of tea with a slice of lemon, the waitress unknown to me. I linger as long as good manners allows and leave her a nice tip. Outside, I walk the grates along avenue and street, my hands at work, my mind at rest. What's this? I see a chalk outline on the sidewalk of a contorted human form, arms and legs akimbo, the desperate jump from a ledge high above still screaming out agony into the still night air.

The fate of such a soul for eons past is to await rebirth in the anteroom of the astral, a ghost, a shade—impatient and suffering for long, long Earthly years.

Okay, I see it—let's shorten the time by clever decree, a few reworkings of how things will be. The Compassionate One now addressing a need, penance and suffering shortened. This new thing is so pleasing that my heart sings and I leap over the contorted chalk form. *Meher Baba is with me again.*

The first signs of dawn scoot me back to the Waldorf, the doorman touching his cap, the lobby of warm red and gold so very welcoming that I gleefully sing out a *good morning* to everyone that I see.

The unused bed in 808 finally reaches out its arms to me and I gladly accept its inviting embrace.

A Sunday morning in November, 1981: Room 808.

After a delicious shower, I find clean clothes in my satchel and I oil my boots with hotel hand lotion. I carefully plait my hair and knot my red tie. I can't see my left hand well, which is a sign that my veil is not entirely in place; nonetheless, I feel energized and even strong. What a delight to be done with all this and to get on with the next program.

Although I have no particular agenda, I know exactly where to go and what to do. The lobby is quiet at this hour as I walk to the side entrance of the Waldorf Astoria. The doorman hails a cab and the Russian driver and I have a limited conversation about his desire to better himself, this job a stepping-stone to something grand as he takes college classes at night.

Aha, the lobby of the World Trade Center is open and I wave off my new friend. As I enter, the enormous space between the Twin Towers is devoid of people, but I can feel the intense energy of the world's commerce that hums continually in this spot. I can feel the heavy weight of immense wealth on the floors above.

Yes, I see the spot, as I awkwardly walk on the polished floor, each step I take requiring great concentration and effort. There is an inlaid circle of colored tile at the precise center of the lobby, a mandala of sorts; this is the proper place to stand.

This, my first Earth-based work, consists of a flurry of mudras at lightning speed, my left hand a blur as I raise it up to eye level. How long does it take? A minute at most. What is the intended result? An eventual collapse of the world economy—this is all I understand at the time. This will be the prelude to the next age, the glorious rising of the phoenix, the Age of Aquarius. What a wondrous thought!

As I turn to leave, my stomach starts growling, the first such message that I have received in a long while. I find my way upstairs to a small café and eat a small bowl of strawberries and cream—delight later dampened by horrible indigestion.

Chapter Eighteen
Love Beckons

In this broad earth of ours
Amid the measureless grossness and slag,
Enclosed and safe within its central heart,
Nestles the seed perfection.
—Walt Whitman

It is a Jamaican fellow this time. He says that the bouncy music that runs his taxi is reggae. "You never hear reggae, mon?" He laughs and half turns to me as he winds his way through New York traffic. "Reggae is what your heart wants to sing," he says as we pull up to LaGuardia.

Well, my heart is certainly singing, but my feet don't want to cooperate. My walk is clown-like, each step an effort of will. The difficulty is centered in the internal adjustments that need to be made as I encounter new ley lines that present themselves every 12 feet or so. Each ley within the lines describes three dimensions: visible (gross), subtle (energetic), and mental (causative). The ratio of these three varies a bit within each ley. People who are only conscious of the visible world have no difficulty walking through changing leys—the three dimensions reported to their senses are based on gross physical laws that operate rationally and are very predictable. Souls that are subtle-conscious experience a different version: an exquisite fourth-dimensional reality that is dream-like and beautiful, each ley a treasure of new wonders. Mental-conscious souls experience very little of the visible world and only a smattering of the subtle. Instead, they are conscious of the drifting thoughts of Isa that find semi-rational placement via the other two dimensions. Mental-conscious souls float above the gravitational field of the earth even as they walk upon it.

My current experience is a composite of all three, which makes movement and thinking a superlative challenge. Fortunately, there is a curbside baggage check-in, allowing my walk to the gate to be unencumbered. People greet me as if I am family: "How you doing? Need some help?"

"Naw, I'm fine, just slow—thanks."

Back in Hawaii I had seen the film *Escape from New York*, and this title becomes my theme as I struggle through blocks of changing energetic states, my clumsy feet walking simultaneously in all three worlds, *eight dimensions in all*, but I am stable and getting more normalized with each step. I feel wonderful. I hear Bob Marley singing.

The short plane ride to Myrtle Beach, South Carolina, is an exuberantly noisy one with a dozen tipsy Scotsmen singing their hearts out. Ironically, these golfers are from the St. Andrews Golf Club, the birthplace of the game, and are flying to Myrtle Beach to play the American version of it. Their boisterous good cheer elevates my mood even farther as I look out the window at the Atlantic Ocean and the piney woods down below. Why am I here? It's a good question. The Meher Spiritual Center is located in this unlikely place, tucked in between pancake houses and putt-putt golf courses, 500 acres of pristine oceanfront property with primitive cabins and walking trails—Meher Baba's home in the West. I need to rest and recover; perhaps the center is the place, but I have no reservation and will need a hotel tonight.

With this in mind, I say goodbye to my singing friends and galumph across the tarmac, the scent of southern pine on the breeze, the sun bright with winter intensity, but with little warmth to bestow.

Having never been in the South, my expectations are low: backward, intolerant, collard-eating people living in trailers sums up my mental picture as I carefully exit the small airport and look for a taxi. But, it is beautiful. I see evergreen woods with white sandy soil and feel a gentle sea breeze that greets me outside, a lovely welcome to this land that would, in time, greatly exceed my expectations. No taxi in sight. I walk over to an idling airport shuttle and peek in the open door. The driver has on earphones and is tapping out a rhythm on the steering wheel.

"Say," I yell. He pulls off the earphones, and I hear Bob Marley again. The driver looks at me, blue eyes wide open in surprise.

"Yeah?"

"You going to the Hilton?" I ask, not really certain that there is a Hilton in this small beach town.

"Yeah, hop in," he says. As he gets out to help with my suitcase, I see that he is about my age but shorter than I, with close-cropped hair and medium build. His movements are rabbit-like and, when he smiles at me, I recognize him. "Jere," he says as he sticks out his hand.

"Richard."

I sit behind him, furiously working mudras for a time before I move to the front seat to his right. "Say, Jere," I begin, as he looks my way, "I need a car and driver for a month or two while I recover. Interested?"

"What, a stroke?" he asks, noticing my odd speech.

"Sort of. I can't pay much, though," I reply.

As we pull up to the Hilton, I see the blue waters of the Atlantic sparkling in the sunlight, the hotel right on the beach. There is a placid lake to the left of the Hilton, the entire scene one of peaceful invitation.

"Sure," Jere finally replies. "I need to give notice."

"Well, you can be part-time for two weeks. How's that?" He nods as we sit in front of the hotel.

"I need to go to the Meher Spiritual Center tomorrow."

"Meher Baba?" he asks. It's my turn to nod, and he continues. "You need to meet Kathleen. She's in Charleston now but stays at the center sometimes." My heart leaps as he says this. *I know, I know.*

Jere Stauffer promises to pick me up the next morning, and I enter the mostly empty lobby. To my utter surprise, the ocean is inside the hotel as well—the ocean of existence. I see the atrium going up eight stories, the roof formed by a glass pyramid. Each floor vibrates with dimensional energy that my open eyes can see, each representing a *pool* as the cascading waterfall of time and events spills from the pyramid of glass above, descending in golden light from one level to the next, shimmering with ever-changing color and hue.

A bellman comes up to help with my suitcase, and I wrench my eyes from this incredible sight. I hear his question drifting to me from distant shores. "Yes, I'm checking in," I say with double and triple *entendre*.

The desk assigns me room 412, the fourth level, the most powerful dimension in the entire array.

So, this isn't going to be a time for rest after all. I'm soon caught up in the electrifying play of God's game on Earth. The elevator ride up to the fourth floor makes my head spin and stomach turn—too fast, I think; the stairs next time.

The room is modern with a balcony that overlooks the vast waters of the Atlantic, a calmer and warmer sea than the Pacific. After a time, the allure of the ocean pulls me out of the room and down the stairs to the lobby once again, which I now see features several shops and a café. One of the shops sells upscale menswear in the same button-down style as Atkinson's in Pasadena. I make a mental note of it and push on to the beach outside. It is very windy and I'm glad for my wool sweater and cap, my boots squishing down the wet sand with each careful step. I notice that my arms don't swing, my walk similar to that of a psychotic on Thorazine. I laugh at the thought; *if this be psychosis, bring it on: I'm wildly alive with bliss and joy coursing through my mind and body*—and I'm not on Thorazine.

I would come to understand that my arms do indeed swing when walking in the more Earthly dimensions, but otherwise, no; so be it.

I soon see a pod of porpoises swimming offshore, their graceful dives through the air reminding me of waterborne angels, which, in fact, some of them are. I acknowledge their welcome and turn to retrace my steps. I don't have enough energy to power much walking and have to stop a few times to rest, just as I did when first walking the pinch in Australia, hands on knees and gasping for breath. I drink in the sea air and feel saltwater enter my blood. I need salt. I need food.

The café in the lobby is not enclosed but is set three steps above ground level on a stage, cut flowers in vases here and there, the 10 tables mostly empty. As I sit, I shake my head in wonder, for across the café, behind a large vase of lilies, I see Jim Sheehy conversing with my medical school mentor, Bill Wright, the two of them world-renowned otologists who were important figures in my distant life as a surgeon in training. Aha! I can now return the favor, as I sit hidden from view, my mudras at work for them personally.

I stare at my cup of tea as they leave, their conversation drifting along with them, talk about technique and research, a nearly forgotten language that pierces my heart with nostalgic remembrance. I order a turkey sandwich and sprinkle liberal amounts of salt on it, the sensation of eating it most welcome. A coke! The sweet tingle of it a reminder that when eating there is pleasure offered up by the senses, temporary as it may be. I seem to be in a rush and summon the waitress and sign the check: R. House, room 412.

"Okay, okay," I say to no one in particular as I slowly walk the stairs to the fourth floor, stopping at each dimensional level for a brief interaction before entering room 412, my current version of an operating theater.

By the time I have situated a chair in front of the sliding glass window, acute nausea comes to visit. (This would be the case for a long while; nausea would bloom after each meal for several years; this the most disturbing part of my daily experience. It gradually abated as I grew stronger and more grounded, but there was no interim relief afforded by dietary vigilance or common remedies. As a member of the profession, I knew better than to take this complaint to a doctor, since my general health was excellent. I simply put up with it in view of my various other oddities that I didn't care to have investigated.)

Somewhere in the wee hours, as I sit in the chair in room 412, I start losing contact with my body, which starts to deteriorate anew. Something must be done. I think about the porpoises swimming in the sea and open the glass door to the sounds of breaking waves below—water, time, and grains of sand are reposing together in a harmonious connectedness that I must somehow rejoin, or perhaps die trying. Is Joe out there?

I wish a good morning to the night clerk, a young man with acne who continues to stare at his computer screen but says hello. I walk outside to the beach. The hotel floodlight sends a cone of brightness that emphasizes the blackness beyond it. The breaking waves have a crest of luminescence independent of the artificial light. I turn to walk along the beach in blackness, imbibing this dim light for nourishment. Meanwhile, my angelic friends out there arrange a means of rescue from my predicament that they send to me in frothy burbles of porpoise speech—a means that I use to tug down my veil farther until I'm better hidden from myself. I collapse on the wet sand and weep, *the loss almost more than I can bear*. I must truly walk in the darkness now.

I'm a sandy mess and spend time brushing off the particles of time from my khakis and sweater. The sun begins its daily program, which gives me hope for the days to come, the rays of dawn peeking above the horizon, my angelic friends of the sea leaping above the water a last time before diving into the depths and departing.

Jere can't get off from work, so I take a taxi to the center, a ride of five minutes at most.

"Oh yeah," the driver says, "I know where it is. It's a nudist colony or bird sanctuary, isn't it?"

"Don't think so," I reply.

I'm met at the gatehouse by a woman named Judy, who is full of calm enthusiasm about everything—particularly about Meher Baba, who stayed at the center three times in the '50s, leaving his divine imprint there, a palpable presence that remains.

"How many nights?" she asks. This question floats in the air while I look out at the tall pine trees glimpsed through the windows of the rustic gatehouse. I look at Judy to see if the proper answer may be found there.

"I don't know." It is now her turn to look at me quizzically, and I realize we are drifting into difficult territory.

"Can we look around?" I ask.

"Sure," she says with some reservation. I'm then inspired to present my Baba credentials:

"I've been to India," I say, to her obvious surprise, "and Avatar's Abode in Australia."

"Oh," she says, her enthusiasm now restored. "In that case, you don't need the usual spiel."

We load into a golf cart and she asks questions that I deflect with well-chosen words, my nausea rising, rising, rising.

Meher Spiritual Center looks like a sanctuary, very peaceful with unpaved roads and natural woods, two freshwater lakes of some size and a long stretch of undeveloped oceanfront.

As the first cabins come into view, I see the peeling paint and sagging roofs of *disrepair*, here and now, here and now. The nausea increases. I turn away from what I've seen. The disrepair is an energetic intrusion of some sort, some malady that needs correction.

"Stop," I say with some urgency. Judy turns to me in surprise, then alarm as I clutch my hands tightly on the dash of the golf cart. I can feel the automatic processes within my consciousness override the malady that so disturbed me. I turn away once again.

"I'm not feeling well." The fact no doubt self-evident. "Please-take-me-back." I'm losing speech and the crows in my worry nest are caw-cawing, fish crows gnawing at my brain.

I stagger out of the golf cart at the gatehouse. "Taxi please," I yell at full volume. True alarm shows in her face as Judy offers to drive me to the hospital, or wherever, bless her heart. "Taxi!" I scream, as I bring down the veil for the last time, as far as it can possibly go.

Jere picks me up at the Hilton the next morning. This time I'm in room 516. I've slept with clothes and boots on, really too weak to think about undressing, so I'm ready to go after brushing my teeth.

"Where to, boss, the center?"

Jere is always upbeat—except when angry—and this day finds him in good spirits as we drive off in his aging sedan.

"No, not the center. Is there an electrical substation nearby?"

"A what?"

"A place where there are high voltage step-down transformers, probably in a chain-link enclosure." I'm exhausted. Finding the proper words is a challenge.

"Oh yeah, I remember seeing one between Highway 17 and the bypass...I think."

"That'll do."

But Jere gets turned around and heads north instead of south. "Man, I'm sorry," he says later. "I never get lost." He laughs and gets us pointed in the right direction. "What's that you're doing there with your hands?"

I really didn't want to get into it. "Uh, energy work, Jere. It's hard to explain."

It takes the better part of an hour, but he eventually finds the substation and parks to the side of it as instructed.

"Switch off the engine now, Jere, and be silent."

I open myself up to the waves of pulsing electricity-borne energy and let it enter. Immediately my body contorts and limbs go taut. My jaws lock open and a soft squeal escapes my throat. My head turns right and I stare at the window lock, my mind entirely blank. It takes about 10 long seconds before it is done, before I slump back into the seat, refreshed. Much like an electrical engine starting up, my thinking brain begins humming again and I look at Jere. He's wide-eyed but calm.

"So, thanks. I'm okay," I said.

"Did that hurt?" Jere asks.

"Not a bit." I clap my hands. "Let's get something to eat."

We drive to Surfside where a café of some repute is located on a fishing pier. Perfect. I order coffee with cream and sugar, Jere a large breakfast with orange juice.

Jere's story comes out bit by bit as we spend a few hours in the café. He had grown up in Lancaster, Pennsylvania, and after college took a teaching position in a troubled high school in Philadelphia. Jere's winning personality and Jewish cynicism was a perfect match for relating to the disadvantaged students who called him Breeze, short for Cool Breeze.

As he's telling me this story, he stands and loudly mimics a black slang greeting, giving me a bump handshake and high five. It is the first time that I have laughed in a long while.

"Okay, Breeze, sit down before we get thrown out."

As it turns out, Jere has recently split up from his girlfriend and needs a place to stay. "Why don't we rent a condo together for a few months?" I suggest, already loving this irascible guy, Breeze, the limo driver.

"Sure," he says with a grin.

While Jere is out looking for a furnished condo, I stay at the Hilton for a few more nights. It would be seven years before I set foot in the Meher Spiritual Center again, by which time the energetic deterioration had been countered but not entirely eliminated.

Each such nexus of higher-dimensional energy is surrounded by negative opposition, which, over time, can erode utility.

This time, I'm in room 311. The third dimension is connected with earth and personal power. As I become more centered, I experience an odd desire that is entirely irresistible: to buy new clothes. I remember seeing the exclusive men's shop in the lobby and am waiting for it to open the next morning.

"May I help you?" the salesman inquires.

"A new wardrobe," I say. He takes in my travel-worn attire and nods in agreement.

Three button-down white shirts, two pairs of gabardine slacks, a leather belt, two regimental-striped ties, a black camelhair blazer, and a pair of black dress shoes does it. I gasp at the bill that significantly depletes my funds, but it needs to be done, needs to happen— *the gentleman doctor has come back.*

The condo in Deer Creek is on a golf course with winter-cheap rates for three months. This will define our time there.

My neurologic function improves day by day, but I still have trouble with speech and walking. Jere is used to it by now, and as I relate some of the recent events, he accepts my disability with greater understanding, and has few questions, his open mind no doubt influenced by his frequent stays in Jamaica, where Rastafarian beliefs grant Ethiopian emperor Haile Selassi godhood and strong cannabis great spiritual worth.

So reggae music becomes the soundtrack for our days in Deer Creek, the lively tempo more upbeat than soothing, cannabis not a part of the equation.

It isn't long before Jere admits a fondness for alcohol, wine in particular: "Nope, Jere, no alcohol." I look into his persona and see great troubles coming his way if he drinks. "On the other hand, if you don't drink for a year, your addiction will be broken. That's a promise."

"Okay, boss."

Although my veil is firmly in place during this period, I can help people in extraordinary ways and do so from time to time. I can also see into the infrastructure of things in general, an example being businesses we pass by on Highway 17. I can look at a storefront and decipher its workings: profitable, or not; worthy products and service, or a business to be avoided—the same open sight that allowed me to see the deterioration at the Meher Baba Center. This ability stays with me for a few months before disappearing for the most part.

Because the visible world is simply the lowest arc of higher energy, I do find it possible to work backwards into causative levels and modify outcomes—*starting with what I see*. A fair example of this takes place during one of our morning walks on the beach. The pleasant sounds of squawking sea birds are suddenly overwhelmed by the thunder of two fighter jets flying low overhead.

"What are you doing, boss?" I hear as I stand looking up at the jets, mudras in full force. There is an Air Force base a few miles away, giving me the opportunity to work with the jets quite often.

"Ah, I'm toning down a high probability of thermonuclear war," I say to Jere as we continue walking along the scrim of wet sand. "It may still happen, but not for quite a while." Jere looks at me with raised eyebrows but has no comment.

When there is an alteration in sanskaric determinants, it usually has other consequences. In this case, one of them was the eventual closing of the Air Force base in Myrtle Beach, which hurt the local economy—a reasonable price to pay in view of the alternative.

A month passes, and I'm solidly on earth again, requiring fewer chargings at substations, and my body is processing food better, though still with nausea. I wear my new clothes now and then as Jere and I meet with some local businesspeople about investment opportunities—a charade that has great purpose but little promise. Jere gets a big kick out of it and eventually becomes a partner in a real estate development project—condos on the beach.

The day shines bright with promise as Jere and I sit in the café at Surfside a few weeks later.

"Okay, Jere, let's go see Kathleen in Charleston." He smiles and gives her a call.

Jere drops me off at the French restaurant where Kathleen works as a bartender part-time, while he heads off to visit friends. "Back in an hour, boss. Keep the weird stuff down."

I flip him a one-finger salute, which makes him cackle as he drives off.

Marianne, the sign outside says. Inside, it is dark and smells lightly of garlic and wine. There aren't many patrons, a few sitting at the bar where I ease onto a barstool, heart pounding. Why? Because I already sense Kathleen... She walks over to me and smiles, extending her hand over the bar. "I'm Kathleen," she says.

With shoulder-length brown hair, and bright blue eyes, she's beautiful, and her voice gentle. *What's she doing tending bar?* I wonder.

"Richard," I manage. "Ah, how about a glass of ginger ale?"

Jere jumps up on the barstool next to me. I can't believe it's been an hour already.

As her duties have permitted, we have swapped enough heart words to come up with a plan: she'll drive up to our condo in Deer Creek on Monday, her day off, to see about all this—maybe a picnic lunch, I suggest.

No, I don't see our unborn children in her eyes, but I am certain that we are beginning a beautiful dance, a *pas de deux*, the Maestro raising his baton in the expectant silence, the orchestra in place, waiting.

She's late. I'm always early and expect other people to honor timeliness as a worthy virtue. Mostly they do...sometimes not, giving me the opportunity to develop patience. As the third hour passes, my store of patience is sorely exhausted. I go upstairs to my room and change into my khakis and blue shirt, grumbling to myself, when the doorbell finally rings. She decided to come after all. I can't say that I find fault with her hesitation: *Who is this man that has stormed into her quiet life?* Who indeed.

Kathleen is bright and cheery as she comes through the door with Leonard, her doggy companion of many years. Having never married, Kathleen has kept a low profile in life, quite content to accept what comes to her rather than pursuing some ambitious goal or accumulating wealth or position; a few good friends are enough for her—and, of course, Leonard, who happens to be a female mutt of some sort, and a very likeable one.

Kathleen was born in an antebellum home in Charleston in 1953, her father, John Harris, a construction superintendent, her mom, Gloria, a nurse. With four brothers and two sisters, Kathleen had ample opportunity to develop survival skills and fend for herself, the quiet one in a boisterous family of hardworking bluegrass pickers, her father never without his harmonica.

It would take quite a while to pry all this information out of taciturn Kathleen, but I am quite persistent. She, on the other hand, has little curiosity about my past, the telling of which dribbled out on a need-to-know basis throughout the months to come. On that very first visit in Deer Creek, a thing of great sadness occurs. Because she's late, our picnic lunch becomes dinner. The three of us have had a grand time, and I invite her to overnight in the spare bedroom.

Early the next morning, I'm downstairs in the kitchen when I hear Leonard's labored breathing close by. I look over at her and can tell that she will soon die, that it is her time. I awaken Kathleen, who rushes downstairs to cradle Leonard as her beloved dog companion breathes her last.

And so our life together begins, Kathleen and me.

Afterword

There is always more to the story, no matter where the telling of it ends.

I would discover that gentle Kathleen, the mother of our two children, is actually a veiled fourth-plane saint.

As you can imagine, dear reader, the years that followed were extraordinary ones. We traveled the world and almost settled in New Zealand, but the Maestro kept us moving. We lived on both coasts of America and visited most of the states in between.

We raised a family that included Megan at a distance, and watched the World Trade Center tumble like a house of cards, the suffering and pain difficult to bear.

Suffering remains an integral part of human experience on earth. Will it always be so? The answer to that question bears close examination and requires more than these pages can offer right now.

♦

I, for one, like *happy endings* when watching Hollywood movies. I favor *romance* and cheerful songs raised to the heavens above. So does God, I think, and His angels that sing of glories to come.

Stay tuned.

As for the players in our little drama, I called my mom two years ago, while her mind was still functioning well, and asked her, "Do you remember when I used to call myself Ichen?"

"Oh yes," she said, chuckling at the thought. "You also wanted your pillow cooled in the refrigerator, your head was always so hot."

I didn't remember that last part, but I'm glad she can laugh about it now. Clearly, my life has been a bit unusual, but the people around me have never failed to give support, including cool pillows.

Steve Keiser is a successful dentist and car restorer, sending me photos of his latest projects. In 1992, he came out to visit, and as we stood in the hand-built cabin where I was living at the time, I grabbed his arm. "You know, Steve, one day I'm going to have one hell of a story to tell you."

Here it is, Steve.

Denny Landsman, my tap-dancing college roomie, and his wife, Kathy, founded the Kansas Regional Ballet Company in Kansas City and are still active in the world of dance.

Catherine did use her master's degree to good advantage, rising to chair of the department of dance at the University of Missouri, Kansas City, and held that position for many years.

Slim and Gabe are still together, their health food store in Montecito still paying the bills while dispensing healthy living.

Megan is comptroller at a large construction company while raising two children with her husband, Joe. While she was still in her 20s, she and I spent a glorious week on the Colorado River running the rapids and camping on the riverbanks at night. It was during this time that I could see how brightly her star shines, even as we watched the night sky fill with lesser ones.

Jere Stauffer? Talk about transcendence. He aligned himself with AA and sober living, giving this precious gift back to others. He still drives fancy cars with a grin and a wave, and accumulates interesting life-stories to tell me when we meet over coffee. *Yeah, boss, you won't believe what happened then...*

As for me, I've been practicing the healing arts, doing chakra work through acupuncture for the past 24 years. I tend a small farm with goats and honeybees and actually bring in the wheat with a sharp scythe. You can follow such things on Facebook and Twitter if you like.

In the meanwhile, I hope that this amazing story will leave you with two thoughts: the first is that there is a lot more going on than meets the eye, and the second is that it all has purpose, this difficult Earthly life of ours, and it is all based on love.

Fare thee well, my friend.

About the Author

Dr. House has been practicing medicine for more than 40 years, first as a traditional medical doctor, and for the past 20 years as an acupuncturist utilizing the chakras for energetic healing.

His travels have taken him around the world three times and to most of the United States for meditative and higher-dimensional work.

He lives in North Carolina on an organic farm with his family and enjoys beekeeping and animal husbandry. He holds a second-degree black belt in taekwondo and is proficient with the longbow. Dr. House may be followed on Facebook and Twitter.